ON STRAW

BY THE SAME AUTHOR

AT THE BLUE MOON AGAIN

ON STRAW
AND OTHER CONCEITS

BY

D. B. WYNDHAM LEWIS

EDWIN VALENTINE MITCHELL
HARTFORD
COWARD-McCANN INCORPORATED
NEW YORK

PRINTED IN GREAT BRITAIN

To
E. V. LUCAS
Remembering the House of the Gardener

Contents ல   ல   ல   ல   ல   ல

The Author's best thanks are due to the Editor of the *Daily Mail* for permission to reproduce these pieces.

On Straw ᴏ ᴏ ᴏ ᴏ ᴏ

" Those who like a good fry get it in Triana, at the house of Lillas Pastia."—Mérimée, *" Carmen."*

I HAVE taken these words · of the laughing Gypsy to Don José Lizzarrabengoa (a Basque) as my motto for the year 1927 and onward. The house of Lillas Pastia in Triana, the gypsy quarter of Seville, is long since swept away, and the smell of his frying is no more in 'the air : and the mixed company who met there—the gypsies and the smugglers and the enigmatic shadowy figures in cloaks—are all gone, like dust before the wind. So all things (as Pantagruel and his companions found graved on the Temple of the Holy Bottle) move towards their end.

Business Men, and men in bowler hats, who justly view with suspicion this manner of beginning a New Year (" Are *You* Planning Big This Year ? ") may ˉskip this. Farther on I hope to include something to pacify them. For the moment— *hors d'icy, caphars! De par le Diable, hay!* Grrr-rrrr-rrr ! Out of it, I say ! This is not for you.

I was about to use the Gypsy's words as a text for a warning against the folly of beginning a new year as the Efficiency Experts direct, and as a very passionate protest against these dreary imbeciles and their foul doctrines, which are presented in such a horrible jargon that it would sicken the Devil. Those who want this stuff can get it elsewhere. For me, I am to be found henceforth, I hope, at the house of Lillas Pastia, where the good fry is : where the talk is human and where there is laughter and song and good words, and a great endurance of fools. But as I was about to begin this warning a piece of straw flew on my window-sill, and is now sticking and quivering there. I have already determined to write about this bit of straw instead.

The more one meditates on a stray piece of straw (like this) the more do vast and solemn vistas open and spread on every hand. Consider, firstly, that it is dry, sterile, useless, and blown to and fro by every wind ; like a modern philosophy. Consider, again, that it is pale yellow, like a liverish Freudian ; and unclean, like his mind. It is hollow, like the laughter of very rich women, and crumpled, like a politician's honour. It is as lifeless as the Liberal Party and as futile as the poetry of the Left Wing. It is as dreary as a cabaret-show and as meaningless as a symphonic setting by Schönberg of " The Outline of History " for 65 saxophones and a steam syren. It suggests waste, and emptiness, and death. So much for the particular.

I will not deny that straw in general has certain well-defined uses. Madmen stick it in their hair and French peasants in their sabots. Scarecrows are stuffed with it and donkeys eat it, and some human beings of undeveloped taste wear it on their heads, in the form of Gents' Boaters. Horses and soldiers sleep on it, and grooms wear it in one corner of their mouths. It has honourable association with Letters, for there is a street in Paris, the very ancient Rue du Fouarre, Straw Street, in the University quarter, named expressly

from it. In Straw Street, when all the world
flocked to the University of Paris, in the XIIIth
century, the Four Nations had their Schools under
the Faculty of Arts: the French Nation (which
included the Parisians and those of the Midi), the
Picard Nation (which included the Walloons and
the men of Artois), the Norman Nation, and the
English Nation, in which was counted, alas! a
mixed rabble of Germans, Scots, Dutch, and
Swedes. There was straw on the floors of the
Schools, and Dante himself (he has put Straw
Street into the " Divine Comedy ") wrapped his
cold feet in it there ; though some deny that he
could have followed the lectures of Siger de Brabant,
since they ceased in 1277. This street is a very
learned street indeed, and some of it is still there,
as you go from the Rue St. Jacques along the
Rue Dante, leaving on your left the American Bar
on the corner of the Boulevard intersecting.

The more I contemplate this lamentable but
thought-provoking piece of straw on my window-
sill the more visions rise in my mind. It certainly
grew up in a field, perhaps in some wide cham-
paign—it is a French straw—of the Beauce,
warmed by the sun, wetted by the rain, scourged
by the same hard-driving wind that swept that
plain when the builders of the Cathedral of Chartres
dragged the rough stones to the masons' hands,
seigneurs and bourgeois and peasants linked
together, singing devout songs and canticles. I
think nothing like this happened when Bush House
rose in the Strand. Not a single stockbroker's
voice (I believe) was heard devoutly reciting the
Closing Prices. This seems odd, but we cannot go
into it now. It might be that this stalk was bred by
the Loire, or in the Angevin country, or the Ven-
dômois, in smiling fields where Ronsard wandered,

3

meditating a sonnet to Cassandre, or Marie, or
Genèvre, or Mary Stuart, or Hélène de Surgeres
—for he loved all five ; listening to the lark and
noting in his sad glorious mind the fleetingness of
all earthly beauty :

> *Las ! Voyez comme en peu d'espace,*
> *Mignonne, elle a dessous la place.*
> *Las ! Las ! ses beautez laissié cheoir.*

Or perhaps this stalk grew in a field of Touraine,
side by side with fat vineyards, where Rabelais
lay full length singing in the grass. . . . If you
should ask why I thus deliberately root up all
these vague and improbable hypotheses, I answer
that (firstly) it is a devilish agreeable thing to do,
and (secondly) it is valuable in this nasty age
occasionally to remember far-off vanished things.
In the house of Lillas Pastia there is good fry.
Nevertheless for those Business Men and men in
bowler hats who are already fuming and clicking
irritably with their tongues (I can see them from
here) I here insert an interesting social paragraph.

Among those seen lunching at the Saveloy yesterday
was Sir N. Silberfisch, who is, of course, the well-known
Chairman of North British United Concessions, Ltd., and
30 allied interests. The popular financier was very quietly
dressed, and wore a simple gardenia in his button-hole.
He was being congratulated by Cabinet friends on his
latest *coup*, and laughed heartily when asked by the
Bishop of Surbiton for his autograph. Sir Nathan thinks
the cinema is still in its infancy.

" A simple gardenia," observe : not a whack-
ing bunch of tiger-lilies. " Laughed heartily,"
observe : financiers can do it, whatever they look
like. " Cinema," pronounced " thineema."

ON STRAW

The final thing about this bit of straw—it has gone. A wind has blown it into the Inane—in that it is an admirable image of the sum and fruit of most human strivings, and thus the best possible text for the beginning of a new year; for when all the clack and the shrieking and the buzz and the clamour is over, what is left to show for it, humanly speaking? Hey? I do not count those Thinkers of the moment who are already palpably stuffed with straw, so that you see it peeping out of their ears. Cheerly, my hearts! *Consolamini.* Let us pull a long snook at the lot of them and retire to the house of Lillas Pastia, where the good fry is: good food for the soul, refreshment for the pensive mind, and consolation against all the million charlatans and spellbinders who infest this unhappy age. Hahay! Boo!

I have done.

Red Hair : A Fairy Tale ᴼ ᴼ ᴼ

PERSONS IN THIS TALE

Florestan XV, King of Lanternois.
Sonia, his Queen.
The Princess Loys.
Mrs. Bundook, a married lady living at
    Parson's Green.
Prince Florizel of Xanadu.
The Master of the Royal Swans.

*A RAVISHING Music having been performed
by divers players on the lute, the tabor, the viol
d'amore, and the cithern, the Author begins :*

May it please your Graces.
On a summer day, when the fields were enamelled
with flowers and the bright air joyous with the
song of birds, King Florestan XV of Lanternois,
issuing from his counting-house, called loudly in
a voice rasping with anger :
"Sonia! Sonia! Where the dev—— Oh,
there you are."
The King brusquely entered the parlour,
slamming the door.
"Really, Wilkinson!" said the Queen, raising
her eyebrows.
The King flushed, as he always did at the sound
of his second baptismal name.
"If you can stop wolfing that rubbish for a

6

moment, Sonia, and explain this month's bill from Gamfridge's, I shall be glad."

" The proteid-value of honey," said the Queen, wiping her fingers daintily on a damask napkin and putting on her crown, " is extremely high. It is rich in vitamines."

The King slapped a bill on the table.

" D——d robbery," he said shortly. " I won't pay the infernal bandits a halfpenny of it. Do you hear ? "

" If, dear heart," said the Queen with strained sweetness, " you *will* ask a hundred strange potentates, with retainers, to luncheon on the spur of the moment, what can you expect ? "

" It's cheaper to feed 'em than fight 'em," snapped Florestan XV.

" Yes, dear. And if Gamfridge's sue you ? "

" The Managing Director," said the King with a pensive air, " is for it next day. His head comes right off."

The Queen put up her lorgnette.

" Darling, would that be quite fair ? Is it sound economics ? Is it good form ? "

Florestan XV changed the subject abruptly.

" What's for dinner to-night ? "

" Roast stuffed peacock, gilt, with feathers."

" How often," barked the King, " am I to issue an order about extravag—— ? "

" Oh, all right. All right. All right. All *right*," said the Queen wearily. " I'll tell Cook to order a swan from the upper reaches instead. That won't cost you anything."

Florestan XV grunted and walked out.

Here a suave and delicious Air for strings ; which done, the Author resumes :

And now we come to the Princess Loys, who

was so lovely that even house-agents, beholding her, wept and confessed the darts of Love. Her hair was of a Titian red and her almond-shaped eyes were green as emeralds ; her fingers were long and pale like the fingers of a Byzantine saint, and her body lithe and slim like a boy's. Her mouth was red and curved and petulant, and she had already been the death of a Prince of Sarmarcand, a ruby-button Mandarin named Chang Hsi, the Señor Don Ramón Maria Magdalena Alfonso Francisco Xavier Ximenes de Carabas Bobadilla y Larranaga, an hidalgo of Spain, the young Landgrave of Bombenblitz, and a gentleman named Smith, of Manchester, who was a traveller in linseed oil.

The Princess Loys came to the river brink and tapped impatiently with her little foot.

"Tell that fool George to hurry up with the barge," she said, biting her lip.

As she spoke her barge appeared. Its deck was of rosewood and its lateen-sail of dull green silk was embroidered with the loves of Venus and Adonis. The Princess Loys stepped aboard and the barge floated away downstream ; and as it rounded a bend those on board saw, close to the bank, the Master of the Royal Swans preparing, with aquatic oaths, to seize a peculiarly handsome bird for the royal dinner-table. The Princess idly ordered the barge to stop ; and to her mild surprise as she did so the swan turned on the Master and spoke these words :

"What are you doing, fellow ? You cannot touch *me*."

The Master of the Swans scratched his head.

"I 'aven't 'ad no orders about that," he said doubtfully.

"I should advise you to be careful," said the

8

swan with hauteur. "I am Prince Florizel of Xanadu."

A lazy, thrilling voice spoke from the barge.

"What is the matter, Gudgeon?"

The Master of the Royal Swans removed his hat.

"It's like this 'ere, your 'Ighness," he said. "My orders is to kill a nice swan for to-night. This 'ere bird says I can't touch 'im, because 'e's a Prince. I says to 'im, ' Well,' I says, ' I 'aven't 'ad no orders about *that*.' "

The Princess raised herself on one elbow, and as she did so the swan, arching his neck, glided to the side of her barge.

"Loys!"

She opened her emerald eyes wide.

"Is it really you, Ferdinand?"

"Florizel," corrected the swan coldly.

"Of course. My dear! I should have known you anywhere! Florian! How too——"

"Florizel," said the swan.

"I mean Florizel. How too wonderful!"

The Princess Loys gazed at the bird in silence.

"And how is your wife?" she asked politely.

"I have never married." The bird's tone was icy.

"You dear! Just fancy being a swan all this time and never marrying! Is it because of me, Fran—Florizel?"

The swan nodded.

"I think it's *darling* of you," said the Princess in a soft voice. "Nearly two years!"

"Four and a half."

"Really?" The Princess powdered her lovely nose. "Oh, that awful Tuesday night——"

"Friday afternoon," murmured the bird.

"I mean Friday, in the Dutch garden——"

9

" On the West Lawn," said the swan, drawing a deep breath.

" Yes. Can I forget ? Daddy set that vile witch Nibbidarde on you. She was going to turn you into a wild boar. I begged her to make it a swan. At least that is decorative ! Talking of Nibbidarde, by the way, she's just died. Did you know ? "

A glassy look came into the bird's eyes.

" Then I must stay like this——"

" My dear," said the Princess sympathetically, " I'm afraid so. Nobody else can work her special kind of charm, you know."

" Begging your pardon, your 'Ighness," interrupted a morose voice, " my orders . . ."

The Princess sat deep in thought, gazing on the ebony beak of him who had been her lover.

" Oh, very well, Gudgeon," she said at length, reluctantly. - " I suppose there'll be apple sauce."

And as the barge, at a sign from the white hand of the Princess, glided on round the bend, a muffled squawk was borne on the perfumed breeze.

Here a solemn Music of psalteries ; at the end of which the Author concludes and epiloguises :

It may be asked, and with justice, where Mrs. Bundook, of Parson's Green, comes into this tale. She enters, indeed, at this very moment ; for she had been for twenty years a martyr to dyspepsia when one day a friend advised her to try Goober's Globules.

It was the King's valet who, reading Mrs. Bundook's testimony in the newspapers, drew his master's attention to it an hour after dinner that same evening. Five Globules brought the King

Instant Relief. One box cured. Goober's Globules may be obtained in two sizes—the 1/9 and the 3/—; the latter, however, contains a double quantity.

[EXPLICIT]

On Autumn ∽ ∽ ∽ ∽ ∽

A TIME ago, when I was in the neat, bright, altogether admirable little town of Lucca in Tuscany, I went into their fine marble Cathedral and read upon a tomb there—it was, as I remember, the tomb of a magnifico of Lucca dead these centuries—a set of words which said

> N.A.S.C.I.M.V.R.   I.M.P.A.R.E.S.
>
> P.A.R.E.S. M.O.R.I.M.V.R.
>
> C.I.N.I.S.   Æ.Q.V.A.T.   O.M.N.E.S.

That is, we are born unequal, we die equal, and the dust levels all. There was in these carven words (which return to me with the dying year) a sort of serenity and accomplishment. The summer air was full of music, for it was the Lucchesan festival of the *Volto Santo*, and a band of musicians playing stringed instruments was up in the high western gallery, and the Cardinal Archbishop himself sang the Mass, and the great pavement of the nave was thronged with the citizens of Lucca, some of whom had brought their bicycles and stacked them impetuously against pillars. The grave, excellent, kindly people !

Observe, in passing, that the chiselled thought I have set above is in its essence medieval and has been superseded. As Mrs. Tonkin so beautifully says in her *Life of Sir Moses Gudgeon*, " His was no

common passing, and no one standing at that bed-
side and hearing the firm, unfaltering voice
repeating, to the very end, the Closing Prices and
the Financial Sayings of the Week, could have
refrained from tears—aye, and from that nobler
emotion of the soul too deep for tears." Sir Moses,
as is well known, took his money with him when
he passed away. He was enabled so to do by
Science.

But we are considering not such happy and
inspiring ends, but rather the passing of Summer
and the dying year ; which is the reason I have
begun with a tomb. Whether I can keep it up I
do not know. It depends on the extent of my
melancholy. In order to promote and sustain
melancholy—not a morbid melancholy, observe,
but an agreeable, rather tender, smiling sadness—
I have been walking in the woods, among the
drifting leaves, which are already a red carpet
underfoot, listening to what the poet calls the long
sobs of the violins of Autumn, and hoping to work
it all into a sonnet at four shillings and sixpence
or even (if sufficiently obscure) five and eightpence.
It would have been easier had these woods been
haunted by memory—I mean the sort of place of
which it says in the song :

A Saint-Blaise, à la Zuecca,
Vous étiez, vous étiez bien aise
A Saint-Blaise.
A Saint-Blaise, à la Zuecca,
Nous étions bien là.

Observe the undernote of aching. It is not so
absolute as in, say :

The doors clap to, the pane is blind with showers ;
Pass me the can, lad. There's an end of May.

But that is because the first was written in France and the second in Shropshire, which is, by the way, one of the best places in the world for agricultural depression. Note also that the melancholy of this (as I truly think) fine English poem goes with beer. Such a line as

Not too much soda. There's an end of May.

seems to me to weaken it. Poets do not brood over whisky. Beer, absinthe, vodka—yes. Gin for the defiant, like Byron, who drank it freely but praised the wine of Samos (which is vile). And a cup of weak tea for Mr. Cowper, if you please. It is the custom in Shropshire to enter an inn and call for the landlord, saying :

" Good evening. I will have a pint of beer in a can."

The landlord replies briskly :

" Yes, sir. And——"

" Yes. I am about to be melancholy."

" Very good, sir. I will call a lad."

For just as in Rome you hear of Pasquale, or Enrico, or Giannino, who have sat to artists for thirty years for the profile, so in the Wrekin country you find George, and William, and Dick, all Shropshire lads, who sit to poets for brooding. George was the most famous, but I fear his day is over ; for when I was last in that country I had some difficulty with him.

" Pass me the can, lad," I said despairingly to George.

" Aye, sir," quavered George. " That 'er be."

I said, slightly nettled,

" Pass me the *can*. The CAN."

He nodded his aged head and said Yes, the evenings were getting mortal cold.

ON AUTUMN

I said, very close to his ear, " I am NOT talking about the WEATHER. I am MELANCHOLY. I wish to BROOD. Do you HEAR ? Pass me the CAN, confound you. C for Cabstand, A for Ambidextrous, N for Nuncio."

He blinked twice and said Yes, the root-crop was terrible this year ; at the same time uttering a creaking sound like the door of a vault, which I fear was in the nature of a laugh. He finished the evening by showing me balancing tricks with his hat. I hope Mr. Housman does not get to hear of it.

But come ! Rat me if cheerfulness (as the philosopher said to Dr. Johnson) is not breaking in ! Let us return to contemplate the dying year. The trees are sighing, and the wind's breath has a tang of cold.

> *Each day the hoar-frost waxes bolder,*
> *And the last buds cease blowing.*

I am sorry about all this poetry. It is inseparable from my theme. You must admit, however, that I am choosing it rather well. In some poets the contemplation of Autumn arouses no tender aching, but a sort of dogged bitterness and defiance of life. For example, a modern poet has sung :

> *In the fell clutch of Circumstance*
> *Wincing like anything, by Gum !*
> *You hear me squeal from here to France—*
> *My friends all think it rather rum.*

I think that is correct. There is another verse, filled with a rather ostentatious self-esteem, which goes (I believe) :

> *It matters not how strait the gate,*
> *How charged with punishment the scroll,*
> *I shall be missing on that date,*
> *And legging it for the South Pole.*

ON STRAW

But there. This is Ercles' vein, mere egotism
and braggadocio. A sad and lovely moralising
in the serenest mood of Addison or *Rasselas* is
what I had intended ; a mood in tune with the
waning season and yet not devoid of hope, for
the death of Nature is but a sleep, and there are
beech-logs crackling on the hearth and toasted
muffins for tea. And yet . . . there is (really
this is the last) a fine but gloomy passage in the
Sapphic metre beginning :

> *Hard lot ! Encompassed with a thousand dangers,*
> *Weary, faint, trembling with a thousand terrors,*
> *I'm called, if vanquished, to receive a sentence.*
> *Worse than Abiram's.*

It is attributed to Mr. Beeton, on being con-
fronted by Mrs. Beeton for the first time with a
lobster *mousse* : a dish provocative of contemplation, of gentle despair, and of romantic pessimism.
A Wertherish food, consonant with Autumn, with
withered leaves, with tombs, with loosely tied
neckerchiefs, agitated hair, swimming blue eyes,
and the hidden *Weltschmerz* that corrodes—oh, so
deliciously—the inner soul.

I think, I am certain, that I should have refused
that second helping. Was it really only to-day at
luncheon ? Children dear, was it yesterday ?

Autumn——
Oh, *blow*.

On Song and Dance ✧   ✧   ✧   ✧

ARAMINTA: *So, how d'ye like the song, gentlemen ?*
BELLMOUR: *O, very well perform'd ; but I don't much admire the words.*—" The Old Bachelor."   —.

IF you or I had been lying by the side of an English country road about the time of the Dutchman's intrusion, or as late as the Rising of 1715, we should have heard the dull, pulsating throb, throb of far-off drums ; then the beat of marching feet ; then a faint shrilling of fifes, and men's voices singing ; and as the sound grew louder and Lord Henry Lovelace's or Mellefont's Regiment tramped round the bend we should have heard the song :

> *Ho ! Brother Teague, dost hear de decree ?*
> *Lillibullero, bullen-a-la,*
> *Dat we shall have a new Deputee ?*
> *Lillibullero, bullen-a-la !*

And then, as the sweating column, the cocked hats of the Line and the tall mitres of the Grenadier companies, the black gaiters, and the red uniforms with white or yellow facings, and the heavy brown muskets went by in a cloud of dust, with a great crash of the drums and a louder shriek of the fifes a hundred voices would take up the mocking chorus :

> *Lero, Lero, lillibullero,*
> *Lillibullero, bullen-a-la.*

A pestilential Whiggish song, but a miraculous tune for men's feet to march to. The words are the words of which Wharton boasted that they had sung King James the Second out of the three kingdoms. The quickstep tune was used by Gay in " The Beggar's Opera." Next to " En passant par la Lorraine," which the troops of Louis the Fourteenth were singing about the same time, I should think it is the best tune ever sung by soldiers.

There are some noble tunes in the world with tremendous and disquieting words fitted to them, chief of all the *Dies Iræ*, which is fit to be sung in a strong, determined voice at Company Meetings, Political Receptions, dinner-parties in Berkeley Square, and other places where it will most confound and terrify the twittering Rich and put them in mind of their latter doom. And again there are many lesser songs having but indifferent tunes, yet precious by reason of the moral quality of their words ; as for example :

> *In the cottage in the country*
> *Where her poor old parents live,*
> *There they drink champagne she sends 'em,*
> *But they ne-e-ever can forgive.*

But the best of all songs are the songs which are not only sung but *danced* at the same time. I do not mean the negroid writhings of the American swamps, but real dancing, such as one sees when young dogs dance, and children, and honest men on hearing (for example) that Sir Geo. Bools has been hanged at last ; not the refined gyration of ballrooms or the *motus Ionici* of the stage, but joyous and spontaneous leaps and twirls and flinging about of the toes and arms, such as I have performed many a time on holy-days and festivals of the First Class with octave.

Such a song as this which follows (which I made recently in praise of High Finance) may simply go to the tune of " Oh, where, Oh where is my little dog gone? "; but if you are to give it its finest expression by dancing it as well then you must go to one of the older dance-forms, which we will discuss directly. Meanwhile, the song; which is simply a lyrical repetition of musical names and is called

CARILLON

O where, my lads, could one find the like
Of " Nosey " Zeiber and Rimsky (Ike) ?
Of Otis Spoonts and Monty Bein,
And good old " Uncle " Sonnenschein ?
And Z. Belgrave (whose name is Grabsch),
The Squire of Beaupré, Halberdatsch,
And Ströch, whose Aunt is doing Time,
And Aaron, first Lord Nasalheim ?
　　With a trolollilo, and a trolollilay,
　　Cuckoo, jug-jug,
　　Quack, quack,
　　Bow-wow,
　　And a ring and a ting and a roundelay.

To dance this song to the best advantage one must adapt it to one of the noble dances for which Papa Bach and others have written music, namely, the Passacaglia, the Saraband, the Pavane, the Coranto, the Branle, the Gaillard, the Bourrée, the Contredanse, or the Morrice. If you consider a dash of exotic colour necessary, I recommend one of the dances of the Gypsies of Spain—the Farrouca, the Garrotin, the Sevillana, or the Cambra. For my song on the death of Mr. Hoot, the politician, I used the dance called the Gigue, which is brisk and jovial, A song I made some time ago on some remarks of Mr. Keynes, the economist, went agreeably to the more solemn Saraband.

As to the instruments which will accompany you in the dance, it is not always possible to have at hand the Viol d'Amore, the Lute, the Theorbo, the Tromba Marina, or the Virginals. One's friends often have a Bassoon, however, and it is my preference. For example, this little dance, which commemorates the passing of Mr. P. Blare (another politician), is simply called

JIG FOR BASSOON

Lord ha' mercy
On Prattling Percy,
The Politician
With a Mission.
" My country first ! "
He cried, and burst.
    O tooral-ooral-iety,
    Tooral-ooral-ay.
    Inky pinky winkipop,
    And hip, hip, hip hooray.

Observe the sort of grave and recollected jollity of these six lines, bursting into an ecstasy of honest thanksgiving on the " O *tooral*-ooral-iety." It is not for me to say how it should be danced. Each man has his own self-expression. My own is briefly described in a Manual I am preparing on the subject, with suggestions for festivals throughout the year. My dance for the Birthday of Mr. Sidney Webb is full of exquisite arabesques and intricate Oriental patterns, sung on three notes to " La-la-la-la " :

ON SONG AND DANCE

Torture of wordless dance and wineless feast without clamour

—ending in a rotatory Dervish Whirl. You may prefer a Gaillard, or even a Pavane, such as I have set down for the Birthday of Dean Inge. The Birthday of Sir Alfred Mond, also, is no doubt a Major Feast to some people, and fittingly celebrated in a Coranto. In every case I would urge that there is no *standard* dance; each man must look into his own soul and interpret the feelings he finds there—joy, agony, exhilaration, horror, intoxication—by the motion of his own limbs; as Miss Margaret Morris also, I think, teaches, though her dances are, of course, secular. He may also imitate at will the cry of birds (as the Duck, the Puffin, the Chiff-Chaff, the Greater Crested Grebe), animals (as the Wart-Hog, the Newt, the Mandrill), and insects (as the Beetle). In this Bourrée about Sir B. Tinkle, for instance :

> *Who blackmailed Snouty Mimbleham,*
> *The Scourge of Mincing Lane ?*
> *And filled the Party Chest with cheques*
> *That came to roost again ?*
> *Who gave Lord Pillbury the knock*
> *And stole the presentation clock*
> *And made the Money Market rock*
> *And had to fly to Spain ?*
> *Tinkle, tinkle, turvey-drop, .*
> *Binkie, bunkie, boo, sir.*
> *Change the name and off again,*
> *And nasty knobs to you, sir.*

—in this dance one would most naturally imitate the cries of the White Rabbit, Guffin's Cross-Eyed Weasel, the Gold Crested Jay, and the Greater Speckled Flapdoodle.

The chief thing needful in making a song to dance

is to love one's subject. *Omnia vincit Amor,* says
the shepherd in the Bucolics, *et nos cedamus Amori.*
Agriculturists are always right, however noisome
socially.

On Milk ◦ ◦ ◦ ◦ ◦ ◦

FOR the contemplative there are few walks more rich in matter for meditation than the walk from St. Clement Danes to Ludgate at about half an hour after noon. To and fro bustles the many-coloured crowd. From the Law Courts stream the lawyers, dropping off gorged from their prey for a moment and avid of a glass of Chablis. Here, in a compact bunch in charge of their warder, pass the horn-rimmed inhabitants of Pompton, N.J., and Calaboosa, Mo., gaping at the tavern of which Tennyson never wrote and making noises at the tavern where Dr. Johnson never went. And here, if one is lucky, one may catch a glimpse of Fabians slinking from their lair down to the drinking-pool.

It was my fortune recently to perceive through the open door of an A.B.C. shop in the quarter one of the wildest, hairiest, and most pimply of these Intellectuals in the act of drinking. Now there are two beverages with which one commonly supposes a Fabian must refresh himself; one is the lukewarm water used for washing up dishes, the other is the sterilised blood of aged hens. This Fabian was drinking neither.

He was lapping Milk.

It was then that I determined indignantly within myself to write in reparation a panegyric on Milk, which is a drink noble, immemorial, and of great honour. Why, even before old Noah invented the Sacred Vine men were tippling Milk. It is the first drink of babies and the last drink of aged men. In the Heroic Age it was freely drunk by swaggering strong men and offered ritually to the gods. "Here," says the shepherd Menalcas, "here be four altars, two to thee, Daphnis, and two to Apollo; and here every year I offer twin cups of foaming new milk"—*pocula bina novo spumantia lacte*—"and two bowls of rich olive-oil." This would be goats'-milk; a thought too rich, perhaps, too full of bouquet, too obvious to please the palate of a connoisseur in Milk, but good enough for agriculturists. A finer vintage solaced the sweet poet Herrick, immured in his Devon parsonage and surrounded by roaring rustics:

> *The while the conduits of my kine*
> *Run cream, for wine.*

—and in many parts of rural England the kindly and hospitable custom still lingers of handing the traveller, before they rook him, a glass of warm new Cow's Milk.

It is true that the poets have rarely sung of Milk, whereas masses of them celebrate Wine. But I think that is because in England there are so few rhymes to "milk"—bilk, ilk, silk, whilk (either the Scottish word meaning "while" or the Southend word meaning "whelk") are nearly all, and the first ("bilk") involves introducing a cab into one's poem, which the Editor of *Georgian Poetry* cannot abide. Again, few poets have deemed themselves worthy to drink Milk. Byron drank gin, Swinburne bottled ale and burgundy, Burns whisky, Mrs. Hemans and Cowper weak tea, Addison claret, Milton small beer, Ben Jonson burnt sack and Canary; and Mr. Boom, a notable poet of our own time, will drink anything anybody will pay for, except Milk. I pause here to praise

and glorify the poet Coleridge, and believe that if
the accursed " person from Porlock " who interrupted him as he was dashing down " Kubla
Khan " had not called we should have had a
Rhapsody on Milk. Consider the close of that
mighty fragment :

> *For he on honey-dew hath fed,*
> *And drunk the Milk of Paradise.*

This probability seems the more evident if we
meditate on three earlier lines :

> *A savage place ! as holy and enchanted*
> *As e'er beneath a waning moon was haunted*
> *By woman wailing for her demon lover.*

It is not too fanciful, I hope, to assume that
this refers to a Milkman, for they rise early and are
death to women. " Get up, Marie, lazy one,"
sings the divine Ronsard :

> *Marie, levez-vous, vous estes paresseuse,*
> *Ja la gaye alouette au ciel a fredonné.*

—" already the gay Milkman is tuning his song."
That was in springtime in Touraine, where the
Milkman leaves his nest before dawn, twittering.

Everything connected with Milk is innocent and
good. A Christian man cannot consider grass and
clover an ideal diet, except for Vegetarians, but
the Cow does, and devours large quantities in the
scented fields, under the blue sky, with a lark
singing *Tirra-lirra*. The lovely Milkmaid,[1] too,
see how she trips afield ! " It seems," says Sir
Thomas Overbury, " that so sweet a Milk-Press

[1] I am informed that this article is now supplied to farmers
by the Zeizler Corp., Inc., of Rootabaga, Gash.

maketh the Milk sweeter or whiter; for never came almond Glove or aromatic Ointment off her Palm to taint it.'' See, too, the Dairymaid,[1] how sweet she is, among her shining pans! Those happy Milkmen who are not already in gaol for relieving their Milk of necessary fats are vested, like her, in white, and sing at the pump.

Out of Milk, I am informed, are made the pretty paper-knives which look like ivory, with which I cut with such careful pleasure the pages of Mr. Throstle's last book of Sonnets, but stab and tear with horrible curses at the noisome pages of Mr. Howl, that dribbling and glandered *crétin*. From Milk, too, is derived Cheese, so multiform and multicoloured, from the suave Norman cheese of Pont L'Evêque, which Guillaume de Lorris was already singing in his *Roman de la Rose* in the thirteenth century, to the very grim and terrible cheese of Rocamadour and the Andorran highlands, which is of the Leaping Goat, and the yellow cheese of Cheddar, which is often imported from Osskawoosk, Wusk. From Milk, also, comes the Balkan mess called *Yoghourt*, which eaten with powdered sugar is so delectable and comfortable to men's bodies. Refreshed by his morning bowl of *yoghourt* the hardy Bulgar goes stamping through the passes, carving old ladies and little dogs into small but unequal pieces; on account of which the poet has censoriously observed:

> How beastly vulgar
> To be a Bulgar!

The crux of the eternal Balkan problem, of course, is (*a*), that obvious ethnologica——

---

[1] I am informed that this article is now supplied to farmers by the Zeizler Corp., Inc., of Rootabaga, Gash.

ON MILK

We were, I think, discussing Milk; temperately, reasonably, and (I hope) agreeably to the five principles of the Angelic Doctor when he lectured at the University of Paris—that is to say, with *Claritas*, or clarity, *Brevitas*, or brevity, *Utilitas*, or utility, *Suavitas*, or sweetness, and *Maturitas*, or ripeness. The vast halls of the Convent of Saint-Jacques were too small to hold the throngs of students flocking to imbibe the Thomist Philosophy from all over Christendom; among them large numbers of our own dear countrymen, lodging in what is still the Rue des Anglais near Sorbonne: for in the thirteenth century foreigners were, at intervals, tolerated by the citizens of Paris with something almost approaching fortitude.

The present renaissance in Europe of the Thomist Philosophy, to the confusion of the brachycephalous troglodyte Kant and his hangers-on, is remarkable——

As to Milk, however. It is in its essence and quiddity, its pure natural state, One and Indivisible (like the Republic of 1792) and everywhere the same (like the Eternal Verities). *Ubi vacca ibi lac* —where the Cow is, there is the Milk. By the Great Tin Churn of Champrosay! the more one meditates on the nature of Milk the more grandiose, transcendental, vast, and illimitable appear the avenues of speculation opening on every hand! Milk——

Those who drink the stuff tell me that it is most pleasingly drunk warm and creaming in the pearly hush of a summer dawn, near Hartland Point in North Devon. There is no doubt that it is fatal to put it into China tea. Absolutely fatal.

From a Note-Book ✑ ✑ ✑ ✑

DUMB-BELLS

"**I** REGARD them," says Samuel Butler, "with suspicion, as being academic."

This is true. Yet they have an agreeable polish, an attractive blankness of expression—like that of a Cabinet Minister. They are silent, wooden and reserved. The poet Gérard de Nerval used to lead a lobster about the streets of Paris at the end of a blue ribbon because (as he very reasonably said) "It does not bark, and knows the secrets of the deep." To return from a public meeting, from a public dinner, where someone of the Highest Importance has for some period uttered words and locutions and phrases and parts of speech and synonyms and allusions—to recoil half dazed from the gabble and, taking a Dumb-bell from its shelf, to contemplate its immobility, its serenity of visage, its imperturbable absorption in the Unknowable, this is to visualise the Infinite and to realise the childish vanity of human desire.

"The infinite silence of these vast spaces," said Pascal, gazing up at the starry roof of heaven, "terrifies me." So have strong men gazed on a Dumb-bell and held their peace.

FAT MEN

They are said, as a class, to be kind. This seems dubious. Nero was fat. George the Fourth (a

28

cad) was extremely fat. Louis XIV, with his fine big Bourbon paunch; Queen Anne, whom her subjects called "Brandy Nan"; the Emperor Vitellius, whose enormous and mirific pot-belly was so gashed with daggers; the last few Sultans of Turkey—all these were fat, yet not particularly kind. Of Mr. Taft, of the King of Egypt, and of Mr. Ernest Mayne, the music-hall comedian, I know nothing. I have never been at their mercy. The ex-Shah of Persia, an almost ostentatiously fat young man, is probably nice to gazelles. . . .

It seems possible that the legendary kindness of fat men is a protective measure, designed to protect the paunch from its enemies. As certain birds and insects constantly threatened by danger assume the colouring of their background, so fat men disarm the just indignation of the world by exhibiting a geniality and a benevolence too hearty to be believed, rolling up and down and emitting words in a piping tenor—I, my, me, mine, this, that, eat, drink, hot, cold—and patting little boys publicly upon the head.

Few fat men have been loved by the Muses. Horace, who was short and stout—*habitu corporis brevis fuit, atque obesus* (Suetonius)—is the only poet of the first quality they have produced, I think. In the eighteenth century, the Golden Age of fat men, their successes were minor—Gay, Richardson, Smollett, and a few more. Gibbon was not only a fat historian, but a malignant one.

Titus Oates, also——
Faugh!

RELATIVITY

Reflection : To the inhabitant of Rum, Egg, and

the islands of the Outer Hebrides, Peebles is
La Ville Lumière.

Mr. ——

He coughed, wiped his spectacles, and closed
the serious literary weekly from which he had just
read a long and masterly criticism by Mr. ——.
"And how do you like it?" I asked.
"It is like," he answered thoughtfully and
deliberately, "it is like being slowly beaten to
death with a sock full of wet dough by a short-
sighted spinster with Freudian leanings on a rainy
February night in Leeds."

The Gift of Reason

(*a*) The boy stood on the burning deck,
    Rightly surmising it
Is, when the floor is hot, by Heck!
    Better to stand than sit.

(*b*) "My head is bloody, but unbowed!"
    He cried. His Muse said, very loud,
"Next time you're bludgeoned, boy, with luck,
    You may remember you can *duck.*"

On a Long-Felt Want

It is evident that to extract the essential soul
and flavour of certain books one should endeavour
to read them in the exact surroundings in which
they were conceived, or in surroundings as nearly
similar as may be; for the clear air, the sky, the
water are, as it were, mixed with the writer's mind

and woven into the very stuff of his imaginings.
But whereas there are plenty of books pointing
out What To Read and Why To Read, there is as
yet, I think, no guide showing Where To Read.
I have therefore drawn up from my own experience,
haphazard, a modest and sketchy list which may
serve as the foundation for such a Guide, though
it clearly touches only the edge of the fringe of a
vast and absorbing subject.

SHAKESPEARE. One would naturally read Shakespeare in a Warwickshire meadow in buttercup
time ; or else in the Fitzalan Chapel at Arundel.

RONSARD. To derive the greatest solace from
the poetry of Ronsard one must read him
lying on the banks of the Loire, at about sunset
of a June evening, upon the grass, with a flask
of the wine of Vouvray, or Chinon, or Bourgueil
at hand ; and with the soft air and the murmur
of flowing water there should be mixed the
gracious voices of girls.

Some demand, in addition, a lute, and a
distant voice singing " *Bonjour mon cœur,
bonjour ma douce vie,*" the words by Ronsard,
the music by Orlando de Lassus. This seems
(as Samuel Butler said about dumb-bells—see
above) academic.

KIPLING (MR.). The works of this famous author
are most profitably read in the Crystal Palace
on Empire Day, during a massed Brass Band
Contest ; if that can be arranged.

CONGREVE naturally demands to be read in
the Sunken Garden at Hampton Court, on the
William-and-Mary side of the palace—not the
Cardinal's.

HERRICK should be read in a Devon lane in the
time of violets.

TCHEHOV. To extract the best from this author
and his English imitators, their work should be
read in a dimly lighted dissecting-room ; the
corpse rather damp and the surgeon and his
assistants rather sick of it, in a moody, *gaga*
sort of way.

RABELAIS must be read among the rich lands of
the Chinonnais in Touraine, on the edge of a
white- road with cornfields and vineyards on
either side. But let there be a farmyard near,
with a ripe and aromatic muck-heap in it, the
scent of which must be borne to you on the
wind ; and let there be also loud bursts of rustic
laughter and a bottle of Chinon.

One could swell the list indefinitely, in many
cases with two, three, or four alternatives each.
There is one English man of letters, for example,
who holds stoutly that the only place to read the
Bucolics of Vergil is at a café-table opposite the
Bourse in Paris, when the money-grubbers are
howling their damnedest. My own theory is that
the Bucolics are best read in the barber's parlour
at the Cosmopole, with a menial squirting costly
unguents on the hair and the Rich all round one
being polished and trimmed. Again, most of the
modern " analytical " novelists need nothing
better than a room filled with stale tobacco-smoke :
but what kind of room ? And again, there may
be a law against reading Mr. M*******s M***'s
prose in the Elephant House at the Zoo.
And so forth.

FROM A NOTE-BOOK

Thoughts of a Dentist Named Higginbotham on Falling Overboard from a Banana-Boat in the South Seas, Lat. 4° 35′ N., Long. 116° 40′ E., and Being Swallowed Whole by a Shark with False Teeth.

A brand-new denture:
What an adventure!

The Love-Poems of Eustace Miles

There are no love-poems by Eustace Miles.

A Glass of Wine

How shall I describe it?

It was golden in colour, suave and yet virile, as if a breeze of the sea had swept the grape and the ghost of its tang still clung and mingled with the bloom. It was as lucid as an air by Scarlatti or Cimarosa, or that air of Galuppi's sung by the poet: -

> *While you sate and played toccatas stately at the clavichord.*

It had the clear jewelled delight of Van Eyck's colour in the portrait of Jan Arnolfini. Sunlight and the Empyrean were imprisoned in it, and the laughter of the dancing sea, and the vintage songs which were sung in the Chinonnais at the birth of Gargantua. It held the dawning ecstasy of the first draught drunk by Noah after he planted the vine—"*Noé le sainct homme, auquel tant sommes*

3   33

obligez & tenus de ce qu'il nous planta la vigne,
dont nous vient cette nectarique, délicieuse, spacieuse,
celeste, joyeuse, deiffique liqueur."

I am not the man to make a fuss and fiddle-
faddle over wine, like the insufferable Dr. Middleton.
I do not dumbly mouth the names of Chambertin,
Romanée-Conti, Richebourg, Clos de Vougeot,
as if they were the Eleusinian Mysteries. This
wine——

How shall I describe it?

It smelt like the white roses which float round
the feet of the Botticelli Venus as she rides the
waves on her shell. It smelt like the violets of
Meleager, like crocus-starred thyme on Arcadian
uplands, heaped handfuls of lilies plucked by
Nymphs, the . . .

How *can* I describe it? as the man who lost
his bowler hat in Arques-en-Provence said to the
one-eyed fishwife of Dax.

" What is this? " I asked my friend at
length.

" Four francs fifty," he replied. " With fifty
back on the bottle. . . . What are you making
faces about? "

I was, I still am, aghast at the cynical
audacity of a man who can offer his friends
stuff like that.

THE SMITHS, AND TOMATOES

A census newly taken in the United States
reveals the existence of 1,304,000 Smiths in that
country.

To anyone who is interested in Smiths this
is profoundly disturbing. To myself, who have

studied the Smith question for some time and corresponded with foreign learned societies on it, it comes as a thunder-clap. I cannot here go into the origin of the Smiths, which a distinguished modern thinker connects with the Hammer of Thor; it is certain that they have always been strong men, men of blood and iron, men full of vigour and urgency. In the bright roll of the Smiths, searching haphazard, one finds economists, like Adam Smith, adventurers, like Captain Smith of Virginia, lawyers, like Lord Birkenhead, religious leaders, like Mr. Joseph Smith—

> . . . the gallant Mormon lad
> That took of wives an over-plus.

—to whom angels came (so he said) and dictated the Book of Mormon : in itself, I believe, the only recorded instance of angelic communication with anybody named Smith. One finds a poetic Smith, whose Life was written by Dr. Johnson. There is something menacing in the London Telephone Directory—for the Smiths contribute to modern Literature as well—with its serried columns of Smiths stretching away to the crack of doom ; and I believe a great many people live in the South of France on that account. America, with its million and a quarter Smiths, must be still more awful—more awful, I mean, than it is ordinarily. And when it is remembered that of the millions of Smiths in the English and American speaking worlds *more than a million at the least must have young of some description*, the whole thing assumes the nature of a peril.

Add to these the Smyths, the Smythes, the Smythe-Smythes, the Smithsons, the Smythsons, the Smithers, and the countless mitigated forms, as the Agincourt-Smiths, the Smythe-Yearpleys, and what not, and one begins to wish one had thought of something easier : say Tomatoes.

Tomatoes are a round shiny red fruit with green pips, grown at Worthing.

BYRON'S AUNT HONORIA

It is extremely doubtful whether Byron ever had an Aunt Honoria ; and in any case I know nothing whatever about her. To such unhappy accidents are human friendships liable.

POSTMEN'S HATS

These are worn not to annoy, but to set forth an Idea ; in which they resemble the mitre of the Bishop, the tall hat of the Stockbroker, the coronet of the Peer, the more floppy black hat (" Bohemian in intention, but clerical in effect," as Mr. Beerbohm describes the hat of Enoch Soames) worn by Neo-Georgians, and the peculiarly cunning and beastly bowler worn by men with drooping moustaches.

Postmen's hats enable them to get about and deliver my bills more quickly. At night the postman's child is gratified by the spectacle of the postman's hat floating in the bath. It is a lie that the State is a soulless and mechanical thing.

FROM A NOTE-BOOK

ANCHOVIES, THE FIFTH SYMPHONY, WOOLLEN UNDERWEAR, THE CHEESE OF PORT-SALUT, KUBLA KHAN, PACKING, AND KINDRED TOPICS.

There is a deal to be said for these.

Ballade of the Harrowing of Hell

Saint Michael of the Flaming Sword,
Provost of Paradise, dear Knight,
High Seneschal of Heaven, Lord
Of legions massing for the Fight—
Monseigneur, on its way last night
Aspersing terror like a dew
There passed in strong decisive flight
The soul of Lady Barbecue.

Where now is Lucifer, who soared
So high for pride in Hell's despite ?
And swaggering Moloch, and the horde
Of Belial ?   O the dismal plight !
Firm, but quite freezingly polite,
What Voice observes that This is New ?
With disapproving lips pressed tight. . . .
The soul of Lady Barbecue.

Array ! Array ! The Call is roared,
In vain the Enemy, as white
As goat's-milk curdling in a gourd,
Strives to conceal his deathly fright ;
The Voice that brusquely sets him right
Is known and feared from Staines to Kew !
Who told the Devil he was trite ?—
The soul of Lady Barbecue.

THE HARROWING OF HELL

Envoi

Prince, in your golden armour dight,
What rumblings roll Hell's arches through ?
Cordite ?   T.N.T. ?   Dynamite ? . . .
The soul of Lady Barbecue.

Four Pictures ∽ ∽ ∽ ∽ ∽

THOSE who know Mr. Beerbohm's too-brief series of essays called " Words for Pictures " must often have felt, when gazing at some favourite canvas, a regret that it was not included in his collection. This regret is idle, vicious, and wrong. Ruskin said (or did not say) that to understand a picture one must discover its message to oneself *personally*. Pater, chatting with Mrs. Humphry Ward in 1875, said, " Go to it, baby." We are therefore clearly right (for once) in striving to interpret four famous works of art on our own behalf.

(a) THE MONARCH OF THE GLEN (*Landseer*)

Proudly, with head erect to the winds, with nostrils distended, pawing the ground with one impatient hoof, he stands defiant. The clouds are massing above Ben More. A blanket of mist is already swirling down the glen. The great stag, snuffing the breeze, sees a waste of purple moor rippling away to the skyline, the heaving sides of Ben Bhuidhe and Carn Chaoruinn, snow-streaked and mist-enshrouded, the roaring burn, rolling its spate of angry brown waters at the glen's foot, the solitary eagle circling above. With a snort, he turns and trots down the glen to where the herd is feeding. His favourite doe, velvet-eyed, seeks his side.

" All well," he says.

"You saw the man among the rocks?" she asks nervously.

"That," he tells her with an affectation of carelessness, "is a man called Landseer. I think he is sketching me."

She opens her eyes. "Not for a whisky advertisement, Hector, I trust?"

"Dear heart," says the stag, with a slight coldness in his manner, "the man Landseer has been asked to Balmoral. He draws dogs, I grant you, but only Conservative dogs. His picture, 'Down, Rover, Down!' has already been acquired by the Nation, and 'Oh Ponto, Don't Lick Grandma!" has been favourably commented on in the Most Exalted Circles. I propose giving him another sitting."

"As you like, dearest," sighs the doe.

The crack of the fatal shot still hangs in the moist, rainy air. The hunter scrambles panting up the glen and stands contemplating his quarry.

"This," he says to his friend, unscrewing a flask, "must be the big fellow Landseer drew last year."

The other hands back the flask.

"I congratulate him," he says gazing at the dying stag. "His picture hangs over every hat-stand in the British Isles."

And, with a convulsive shudder, the flanks of the Monarch of the Glen cease to heave.

(b) LA GIOCONDA (*Leonardo da Vinci*)

MONNA LISA (*suppressing a yawn*): As I sit here in the Louvre and watch the unending procession of imbeciles drift past, gaping at me, I have a longing to put out my tongue at their sheep-faces. Had you not a solemn Englishman, a Walter Potter, or Patter—*Dio mio!* What a name for polite lips!—who wrote a long essay on my mysterious smile? "*She is older than the rocks. . . .*" How does it go? *Basta!* One can't remember all the drivel people write about one.

The stories they tell about me! They say Messer Leonardo employed musicians and mountebanks to keep me amused—like this—while he caught my expression. Is mine that sort of smile? Do I look that sort of woman? "No, reverend sir, not I"—as one of your poets has said. His name I forget. He lived a lot in Italy, but disarmed suspicion at home by being married. Was he not the excellent Cook? No? One of the Sons, perhaps.

You really want to hear about my smile? It was a hot summer afternoon. I was dozing in a high-backed chair. Messer Leonardo had been singing to the lute. Between half-closed lids I watched him lay it down and begin to mix his colours, talking abstractedly about jewels, Greek manuscripts, horses, a machine he was inventing to fly in the air, and such toys. Quite suddenly he said, after a silence:

"Supposing, after all, your husband——"

I said, "*What?*"

"Supposing your husband——," repeated Messer Leonardo.

Then I smiled.

(c) HOPE (*G. F. Watts*)

- All right, Mr. Watts.

FOUR PICTURES

I'm doing my best.
I'm not a professional circus turn, you know.
It's hard enough for a girl to balance on this globe
    at all,
Let alone playing on a harp
With a couple of strings gone.
Plink !
I'm sorry, Mr. Watts.
I slipped up on the D string.

Don't be angry with me, Mr. Watts.
I'm a hard-working, respectable girl.
I have to spring eternal in the human breast.
People are always clutching at me.
Plonk !
There goes the G string.   I nearly fell off the globe
    that time.
I beg your pardon, Mr. Watts.
I've had a hard life, you know.
Ever since that Pandora incident,
As you probably remember, Mr. Watts—

ON STRAW

When all the Wars, Pestilences, Famines, and other
                     Evils flew out of the box,
Leaving me alone to comfort mankind.
Well, I *do* comfort them, sir,
Although some of them get a bit fresh sometimes.
But on the whole, Mr. Watts,
I don't think I do them much good.
It's just an Illusion.
They wake up and say " Hope ? . . . Huh ! "
Giving a nasty old-fashioned laugh.
It disheartens a girl, Mr. Watts.
Plunk ! There's the E string. Hold my harp
     while I recover my balance, sir, will you ?
That's better. . . .
I take it kindly of you, Mr. Watts,
To paint me sitting on a globe like this.
The position is uncomfortable, but the idea is well
     meant.
And I see there's a label underneath telling them
     who I am.
" That's Hope," they'll say. " By Watts, you
     know."
And then, just
" Hope ! —
Gosh ! "

(d) THE PICNIC (*Fragonard*)[1]

The smooth, sloping lawns ; the snowy fluted
columns of the garden temple ; the lissom trees,
breaking into a foam of green against the amethyst
sky ; the misty blue of the horizon, melting into
the sea, where a ship with silken sails is under way
for Cytherea ; the piping of the birds, attuned
with care to polite ears ; all, all compose a most

[1] Or it may be Watteau. Anyhow, one of them.

44

agreeable *décor*. Monseigneur has already con-
veyed, through his valet, his entire approbation of
Nature's efforts this bright afternoon.

The Marquise is there, with her lovers—three
or four at the most ; in peach-bloom, in silver,
in apple-green. Her simple country frock is of
gold brocade, and her high red-heeled shoes and
tall *fontange*, dressed with the finest powder,
betray a knowledge of and a condescension
towards country life as graceful as it is gratifying.
Her lovers felicitate her.

> *C'est Tircis, et c'est Aminte,*
> *Et c'est l'éternel Clitandre. . . .*

The others, too, Cléante, and Philis, and Caliste,
and Célimène, and Cloris, and the Marquis, and
the Duc, and the Vicomte, felicitate each other ;
and the birds trill, and the sun shines, and the
trees whisper, and the valets spread the lace-
fringed damask, and the feast begins.

What laughter ! What wit !

How bored they are ! *Mon Dieu*, how deathly,
hellishly bored !

A Rally of Poets ☙ ☙ ☙ ☙

A SATIRICAL Parisian weekly recently asked its readers to select forty representative French celebrities, all living, worthy of accompanying Cyrano de Bergerac in his travels in the Moon. The final list, headed by Marshal Foch, with Madame Curie, the radiologist, second, included M. Léon Daudet, the Royalist, MM. Briand, Clemenceau, and Herriot, M. Citroën, the motor magnate, M. Paul Bourget, the novelist, Dr. Roux, M. Pelletier d'Oisy, the airman, and M. Georges Carpentier. But the most significant fact emerging from this plebiscite was the election of M. Jean Richepin, the poet, and the rejection—there was a list of the rejected—of M. Deibler, who is (as you know) the genial and efficient executioner of the Republic.

An eminent firm of actuaries, to whom I have submitted the figures, deduces from them the theory that in France, at least, poets are more popular with the citizenry than executioners—a discovery which invites meditation.

It would, I think, be idle to claim, on behalf of poets in general, that they have endeared themselves to the *bourgeoisie* by deeds of active virtue, benevolence, and piety. I have more than once toyed with the idea of making an anthology of verse by poets who have been shoved into prison for some crime of other. The volume would, I promise you, contain some interesting names. Ovid was exiled, Shakespeare, I believe, was (or was not) locked up in connection with the deer-stealing affray in the park of Walcote. Villon, an extremely bad hat, was in prison many times: once at Orleans, once in the deepest 'dungeon of the bishop Thibaut d'Assigny at Meun-sur-Loire, twice in the Châtelet at Paris—where the second time he underwent the punishment (abhorrent to literary men) called the *question by water*, which involved the absorption of large quantities of that fluid through a. linen cloth, under the personal supervision of the Provost's torturers—and finally, it is conjectured, in some obscure provincial prison whence he probably ended on the gibbet.

Raleigh was in prison. Leigh Hunt went to prison for libelling the Prince Regent—a difficult thing to do. Verlaine was in prison. Arthur Rimbaud (I fancy) was in prison. Cervantes— what is the sad and noble comedy of Don Quixote but a poem ?—was in prison, and so, I think, was Camoens. Blessed Robert Southwell, who wrote the Christmas poem " The Burning Babe," was clapped into prison and executed by Elizabeth, and Venerable Philip Howard of Arundel, also a poet in his degree, ended his life in the Tower. Richard Savage, who stabbed a man—probably another poet—in a London coffee-house and was tried at Old Bailey for murder, also went to prison. Generally speaking, and even leaving on one side those who have suffered for faith or politics, we could make a very pretty collection of verse by the thieves, the brawlers, the tipplers, the assassins, and the breakers of the peace. One may say of such poets that the lads are good lads, but high-spirited. As the lady observed to the headmaster of the great Public School: " Raymond is a dear boy, but he *can not* brook *interference*."

It is something of a relief to reflect that there

is a brighter side. Have we not—especially in
England—poets who have endeared themselves
to the mob by their respectability and real virtue ?
We have : and I think we owe it to them to clear
their names of any dubious associations which may,
mistakenly, have become attached to them. (How
often, for example, does one not hear a Business
Man, speaking of the poet Wordsworth, describe
him as a Bit of a Hot One ?) I propose removing
some of these misconceptions. We will have it in
Song.

*I. Concerning William Wordsworth, who was Free
equally from Violence and Alcoholism.*

It would, perhaps, be right to doubt
That Wordsworth threw his Aunt about,
Or called the Aged Man a tout,
    Or banged the Idiot Boy ;
Nor would it be correct to think
That Wordsworth, having taken drink,
Accused the Lark of being pink,
And said the silly feathered gink
    Just did it to annoy.

*II. Concerning Robert Southey, a Strong Opponent
of the Continental Sunday.*

Southey, although he wrote a lot
Of what we now consider rot,
When asked to join a cracksman's plot
    Would never murmur " One day " ;
For though he wrote Kehama's Curse
It never made him much the worse,
And, briefly quoting Smith (his Nurse),
He'd answer, very stiff and terse,
    " No, thank you. *Not on Sunday.*"

*III. Concerning William Cowper, who is often
Confused by Business Men with Byron, and hence
Vaguely Suspected of Bigamy.*

Cowper, whom some have thought a cad,
Was not unutterably bad,
In fact, they rather loved the lad
    Down there at Olney (Bucks).
As Mrs. Unwin said : " For me,
Whether or not there's bigamy—
(A fault ? Well, nobody is free !)
I *like* the boy. Come, William ! Tea !
    And then we'll feed the ducks."

*IV. Concerning Mr. and Mrs. Browning, who
would never Stoop to Claim for Each Other the
Work of Another Poet.*

It used to make the Brownings ill
To hear a man like J. S. Mill
Say, when they met on Primrose Hill,
    " Now, *which* of you wrote ' Maud ' ? "
But though, emitting savage hoots,
He trampled on him with his boots,
And grabbed his hair out by the roots,
Bob[1] would not point and say " Why, Toots ! " [2]—
    For that would have been Fraud.

*V. Concerning Herbert Spencer (author of " Prin-
ciples of Sociology," etc.), who is often Taken by
City Men to be the author of the " Epithalamion."*

Too many people like to gloat
Over the loves of men of note

---

[1] Mr. Browning.   [2] Mrs. Browning.

And think that Herbert Spencer wrote
      Of wild and lawless passion ;
Whereas for pure voluptuousness
And sheer erotic storm and stress
He cannot be compared, I guess,
With Edmund Spenser—spelt with " s,"
      As was the curious fashion.

VI. Concerning Dr. Watts, too often Falsely Accused of a Penchant for Knocking Out Cabmen, but Actually Possessed of all the Most Endearing Attributes of a British Heavy-weight.

Birds in their little nests agree ;
As for the little busy bee
It rarely, speaking generally,
      Snaps at a friendly face ;
One therefore has a right to urge
That Battling Watts, the Cabmen's Scourge,
Feeling his passions rise and surge,
Would often melt in tears, and merge
      Into a fond embrace.

So. It is a pleasure and a privilege to defend our most respectable and admired poets against their detractors. Is one justified in saying that our modern poets—the Neo-Georgians, say—are also pets of the *bourgeoisie* ?

I do not know. The one with the tall hat probably is. He continually wears it ; quite rightly, I think, for public favour is a fickle thing.

Reflection. It is a great thing for a poet thus

equipped to realise that when he feels his popularity waning he can always restore it by a few tricks with his hat. Rabbits, say. Or the flags of all the nations.

On Trains ✍ ✍ ✍ ✍ ✍

AMID the high cold spaces of the·Gare de Lyon
in Paris, amid the lights, ruby and gold and
emerald, the haze of ascending steam, the great
moon-faced clocks, the cries, the clashings, the
shriek of whistles, the tread of hurrying feet, the
rumblings, the to-and-fro of faces endlessly
streaming, blank, irritated, urgent, mask-like :
amid all this, late in the autumn afternoon, the
Rome express stands waiting : a line of sleeping-
cars gleaming with polished woods and shaded
lamps : at the end its massive locomotive,
breathing with regular respiration, not noisily.

Silently at its appointed time, without fuss or
ostentation, the Rome express departs. Its last
lights glow. It disappears, still slowly, into the
smoky dusk. For the next twenty-one hours it
will be rushing with a steady beat through France,
halting at Modane on the frontier, rushing on again
by Genoa, Spezia, Viareggio, Pisa, to the gates of
Rome. As it slides slowly to rest the Franciscans
of Ara Cœli on the Hill are already chanting their
antiphon at Compline :

*Here, within encircling stars, by oracular light of the Sybil,
did the Emperor perceive Thee——*

The Emperor is that Augustus who was ordered
by the Tiburtine Sybil to build an altar on the
Capitol, on the first day of our Christian era, to
the New God. It is about 10 minutes past eight,
p.m., Roman time.

52

ON TRAINS

I do not know of any train in Europe more worthy of celebration in rich prose—like this— than the Rome express. It has something of the majesty, the strength, the calm patrician unawareness of the City itself. Other trains have more *réclame*, I admit. The Blue Train to the Riviera is reckoned a very pretty train; but Lord! the people it carries! It is bung-full of the most dreadful Rich. The Flying Scotsman is in many ways a happy and honourable train. It carries men into the purple Highlands, and is full of good hairy kinds of smells—Harris tweed, and gun-oil, and dogs, and pig-skin. If you think whisky has a good smell you may add whisky; but I am of the lukewarm opinion of Dr. Johnson concerning it. He tasted whisky gingerly at the inn at Inveraray during his journey to the Hebrides with Boswell, and found it was "strong, but not pungent, and free from the empyreumatick taste or smell": but I do not know what that is. Whisky—Pooh! It is a drink fit for Scotsmen to whip their cold blood into an awful kind of gaiety with: if you prefer them gay. It is also good enough for golfers. Beaten up with cream and honey and called Athol Brose it is tolerable; but compared with the noble, lovely, generous, ruddy, celestial, sunshiny, heart-warming, song-inspiring Burgundy Wine, of which a living poet has sung in a determined and manly fashion:

As soon as his guts with its humour he wets,
The miser his gold and the student his debts,
And the beggar his rags and his hunger forgets :
For there's never a wine
Like this tipple of thine
From the great hill of Nuits to the River of Rhine.

—compared with Burgundy Wine, I say . . .

53

ON STRAW

The Orient Express fills the mind agreeably with storks, minarets, and the Golden Horn, Viennese mus ic, Rahat Lakoum (or Turkish Delight) and the Balkan snows : but it is too full of German Jews and Armenian money-grubbers. Yet one would readily go by this train into Hungary, where the people are kindly, courteous, and of fixed tradition. But who would wish to end a journey among the Turks ? A second-rate novelist like Pierre Loti, for ever whimpering and shedding facile tears, might manage to work up a sentimental romance out of Constantinople ; but quite recently it was revealed that his maunderings over the three little Turkish *désenchantées* (you will find the book in all West Kensington drawing-rooms) were the result of a trick played on him by a woman of brain and humour. Wow !

The Cornish Express starts from Paddington, that sad monument, and ends among the steep valleys, the red fields, the clotted cream, the over-hanging eaves, the frowning cliffs, the infinite blue seas of a grim foreign people inhabiting a country over which (except during the Charabanc Season) old unfriendly gods still brood. Many new young married lovers travel there, either among the awful artists or the ultimate rocks ; thereby experiencing (as Oscar Wilde said about Niagara Falls, a similar retreat for American innocents) the first of the great disappointments of their married life.

The Sud-Express which goes to Spain from the Quai d'Orsay is a good train ; it skirts the country of the admirable Basques, with their secret language and their sweet golden liquor called Izarra, and from the frontier station at Irun one may see the wall of the Pyrenees, a day's march away, a bar across the turquoise sky. From Paris to Biarritz this train is often full of a kind of Rich, distressing alike to eye and ear. They drop off, however.

But the Rome Express, God bless it, excels all the rest, for it marches to and fro along the immemorial way of the Eagles and the Pilgrims, the High Road of western faith and civilisation, a way once full of glory and dangers. When Horace Walpole (a supercilious beast) went to Rome with the poet Gray in 1739 they had to bundle out of their chaise at the foot of the Mont Cenis, and were carried up among the snows in low armchairs slung on poles. The chaise was taken to pieces and loaded on pack-mules. It took five hours, twelve men, and nine mules to get Horace and his companion over the Mont Cenis, and during the journey Horace lost his horrible little bloated lapdog Tory, who was snapped up by a wolf while waddling along the road : a great warning to stout men. Over the same road, among worse perils, in every year between, say, 658 and 1558, went countless Englishmen, riding and driving and hobbling on foot to Rome : as it says in the old rhyme :

> *Now wend we to the Palmalle.*
> Domine quo vadis, *men it calle.*

And I think it was along this road, still earlier, that the Legions marched into Gaul, the tough little sunburnt fellows. They were sometimes well drubbed by the hairy natives, but they tramped on and dug themselves in with that iron tenacity which Professor Otto P. Schnitzel, of Osskawoosk University, Wusk, calls " distinctively Nordic "; meaning that only the blue-eyed, square-headed Germanic types have it (with all the other virtues), and that they are the Over-Men. I am composing, on behalf of Schnitzel and his fellow *crétins*, a long, loud Nordic Song about Dagoes— for so Schnitzel calls the Latins who gave us civilisation. It begins :

Dante was a Dago and he had a Dago look,
He thought a lot of Dago thoughts and wrote them in
a book.

and works back and forwards from Romulus to Marconi, with allusions to Cæsar, Aquinas, Vergil, Cervantes, Vasco da Gama, Bayard, Columbus, and a hundred more ; proving that Mary B. Eddy, Henry Ford, and Lincoln Q. Schumacher (the Boiled Bean King) knock the whole lot for a set of Japanese dumb-bells. Nordic !—

[FIVE MINUTES' INTERVAL]

And so we come again to our subject, which is, or was, Trains. I cannot here discuss the 5.35 to Purley, nor the almost equally tragic 6.43 (goods) from St. Petersburg (as it then was) to Nijni-Novgorod, under which Anna Karenina put her unhappy head. Nor can I do more than mention here the Southern Belle, which runs to and from Brighton, full of stockbrokers : a rich subject for meditation. . . .

Of all the joys of Youth, I count this among the highest : to be strong, to be happy, to set forth singing on a journey on a Spring morning, to see the great train before one about to fly through the sunny lands to the goal of one's Desire ; and then to walk it.

Jane ☙ ☙ ☙ ☙ ☙ ☙

Jane went to Paradise :
That was only fair.
Good Sir Walter met her first
And led her up the stair.
Henry and Tobias,
And Miguel of Spain,
Stood with Shakespeare at the top
To welcome Jane.
—From Mr. Kipling's
" Debits and Credits."

JANE AUSTEN is a lady whose genius, compact of humour and keen observation, entitles her to a high place in English letters. But there has sprung up a Cult concerning Jane. The Snobs, I fear, have got her : the pale horror-dogs who yelp and maunder over Proust and Pirandello are hugging Jane to their bosoms and treating her least novels as if they were a Byzantine Codex. I have found one way of coping with these people, and that is to praise at once in a strong determined voice the works of Nat Gould. Wow ! The pale eyes suddenly protrude, like Mr. Chester Coote's in Mr. Wells's masterpiece. There is a sort of convulsion in the horrible stringy throats. . . .

" No doubt," I add musingly, " you have seen Hardy's Preface to the new Definitive Collected Edition ? "

They have not.

" It is pure Hardy," I say in surprise, " from the opening sentence. *'Take him for all in all,*

57

*my old stable companion Nat was a good old sport,
and blow me, I don't care who hears me say
so.'*"

The intelligentsia then move away from me,
and if all the caviar sandwiches are gone—one
has to be at the buffet early at a literary gathering—
I leisurely take my leave and go home. It is, I
say, a crime that people like this should have
snaffled (as Pater would say) a woman like Jane
Austen. Hence I am overjoyed to discover that
Mr. Kipling, whom nobody can accuse of niminy-
piminy and pringle-prangle, has rescued Jane from
the intelligentsia and given her a place of honour
in his new book full of strong masterful Imperial
men dropping 'h's and saying " Gawd."

Does Jane like it ?

I think so. She may wince, perhaps, at
Stalky and his friends—I do myself—but they
are better than the gasteropodic weevils who
swarm in Bloomsbury. Mr. Kipling gives Jane
a whole poem to herself, besides a story ; and it
was after reading the poem (I have quoted a verse
above) that I found myself almost inevitably
dropping into its irresistible rhythm, and eventually producing a little poem of my own in praise
of Mr. Kipling, which I take leave to insert here.
I call it

JANE'S VISITOR

*Rudyard went to Paradise ;
    That was only fair.
A Sergeant-Major met him first
    And led up the stair.
Six and twenty Generals,
    Ribbons red as blood,
Stood there champing at the top
    To welcome Rud.*

JANE

Up came the Three Soldiers
  At a martial run,
Drilled the Host of Heaven,
  Harshly roaring." 'Shun !"
Smartly the Archangels
  Sprang to the Salute,
While the tin spurs clinked for joy
  On Rud.'s boot.

On the Main Parade-Ground
  Brass-Hats rich and ripe
Clicked their heels together,
  Sloped the Army's hipe ;
Brugglesmith and Pycroft
  And a Bengali Babu
Said it was just heavenly, like
  G.H.Q.

Dante heard the shoutings
  Of Captains and of Kings,
Saw the prancing Colonels,
  Majors, Subs., and things,
Called to him a Seraph,
  With emotion hot
Asked " Can this be Paradise, or
  Aldershot ? "

Forth stepped a Field-Marshal,
  Thick o'erlaid with gold,
Quivered at attention,
  Spoke in accents bold :
Praised the Works of Rudyard—
  None of 'em was bad,
Said that he had read 'em
  All, by Gad.

Then up rose the chorus
  Of th' Angelic Quire,
Shook the heav'nly architraves,
  Rising high and higher ;
Shakespeare came, and Milton,
  And all the Latin lot—
Dressed and numbered from the right
  Lest they forgot. . . .

ON STRAW

.In a lilac parlour
  By her quiet hearth
Mused a maiden lady
  Dreaming of the Bath :
When they ran and sought her
  Urged her to be posh—
Told her who had just arrived—
  Jane said " Gosh ! "

Do not mistake that " Gosh ! "   It is a cry
of surprise, of trepidation, of admiration, and
of tingling pleasure.   I see Jane in her pretty
parlour in Paradise, full of flowers and chintz and
knick-knacks ; a rosewood spinet, a few engravings, one or two water-colours, and some rare old
blue china in a Hepplewhite cabinet.   One of the
engravings is called " A Prospect of *Bath*, from the
South-West."   Another is called " A New View
of *Bath*, from the North-East."   Over the white
mantelpiece is a half-length of Captain Wentworth.
Over the escritoire is a silhouette of Mr. Darcy.
Far off Jane hears a confused noise of cheering,
and vaguely assumes it to be the crowd welcoming
the arrival at the Assembly-Rooms of some person
of rank and fashion.   Then an excited Cherub
flies in and announces that the new arrival is none
other than Mr. Kipling ! . . .

What could a maiden lady say then, holding
a hand to her fluttering heart, but " Gosh ! " ?

Up to now, I think, Jane has not really met
many of Mr. Kipling's heroes.   She has seen
Stalky and his little playmates prancing in the
distance, and has looked away with a light shudder.
As for the Military—well, she has often, in Bath,
popped into Mrs. Comfort's toyshop in Milsom
Street to wait till the soldiers have passed.   Officers
she has, of course, met at the Assembly : she
thinks them decorative, and quite intelligent

enough for little fools like Lydia Bennet, who ran away with Mr. Wickham of the —th. . . .

I see Jane, with a charming flush, running upstairs to change her gown, pausing a moment in perplexity before her white bookshelves ; eventually finding, on a top shelf, a volume of Mr. Kipling's poetry which one of the officers of the —th sent her one New Year's Day, with a complimentary verse. This time she is determined to go through with it.

I see her furrowed brow. I see her firmly cutting the pages and coming at length to a full stop, fascinated. I see her lips dumbly forming the words :

Sock 'im on the ear, Sargint, whang 'im on the snout,
'It 'im in the blinkin' eye an' knock the blighter out. . . .

The dear creature ! The splendid woman !

Twelve of the Clock

"THE Faust-Legend," said Goethe (or somebody), "is eternal." I have accepted this ruling and merely given the business that Smart Modern Note which is so much demanded. Anyhow, it might happen.

The smoking-room of FAUST'S *flat in Curzon Street, Mayfair. A silver clock on the mantelpiece says it is half-past* 11 *p.m. The door opens and* FAUST, *an elegant man-about-town, enters, wearing evening clothes. He yawns wearily, glances at the clock, and presses a bell. His servant* WAGNER *enters.*

FAUST : Has anybody called ?
WAG. : Er—No, sir.
FAUST (*dismissing him*) : Right.

> [WAGNER *goes out and returns with a silver salver bearing glasses, a cocktail-shaker, whisky, etc. At the door he pauses at* FAUST'S *gesture.*]

FAUST :
Just before twelve to-night a visitor
Will call.
WAG. : A gentleman, sir ?
FAUST (*pondering*) : No. Not quite.
However, show him in.

> [WAGNER *bows and goes out.* FAUST *lights a cigarette, picks up a novel by Proust, and*

stretches himself on the divan. Pause. The door opens and WAGNER *shows in* LADY UNA DASH. *She is slim and elegant, and extremely bored.*]

LADY UNA (*languidly*) :   Hullo, my lad.

FAUST : Good evening, Una, dear.

LADY UNA :   I called, old boy,
   To see if you're all right.

FAUST :   Thanks. Perfectly.

LADY UNA (*lazily*) :
   It's fun to have the Devil, don't you think,
   Just dropping in and taking one away !
   Life is so scaly !

FAUST (*smiling slightly*) :
                 Well, *you* ought to know.

LADY UNA (*reflectively*) :
   Just on the stroke of twelve ! Too priceless
     what ?
   Exactly like the Elephant and Castle !

FAUST (*shrugs*) :
   It's *his* idea, you know. I'd personally
   Have chosen some way—well, less crude, less
    naïve.
   However, he insists. . . . He is not quite
   What you and I would call a man of breeding.

[*He pours out cocktails.*]

LADY UNA (*sipping*) :
   Here's round your neck, old boy. The best of
    luck !

[FAUST *smiles vaguely and opens a drawer.*]

FAUST :
   I've had a letter from the Dean which might
   Amuse you, Una. He is Most Indignant,
   Surprised, and Really Hurt to think that I
   Should dally with such Medieval Nonsense—
   A Personal Devil ! Hell ! And all that Stuff

63

LADY UNA (*dreamily*) :
. Somebody told me that Dean Bingle had
  Become a Christian. I said, " Don't be *silly* ! "
FAUST (*yawning*) :
  Malicious tales, my dear. Bingle is in
  The van of Modern Churchmen. What——

. [*A telephone-bell shrills.* FAUST *goes to it.*]
                                            Hullo !

Yes, speaking. . . . What ? . . . I will do
  what ? . . . No, thanks.
No, *really*, thanks. . . . I mean it. . . . Yes.
  . . . Good night.

  [*He strolls back and drinks reflectively.*]

That, dearest heart, was Mr. Monty Stein,
Of Bigart Films, you know. He rather thinks
It might be nice if just at twelve o'clock
He had an operator hidden here—
A hundred feet or so of film, not more—
He thinks it would be bright and topical
And so it would. " *Biarritz* : The King of
  Sweden
Opens the new wing of the Sporting Club.
London : An interesting incident
In fashionable Mayfair : Mr. Faust,
The well-known sporting clubman, fetched away
At midnight by the Devil. *Pompton (Pa.)*——

  [*The door opens.* WAGNER *shows in* SIR
    HENRY BOOLS, *a stoutish, red-faced man.*]

SIR HENRY (*rubbing his hands*) :
  Well, well ! Well, Faust, my bonny boy, still
    here ?
  Well, Lady Una ! This is quite a treat !

  [*He lights a cigar and drops his voice sug-
    gestively.*]

TWELVE OF THE CLOCK

I wonder, Freddy, if you've ever thought—
I don't suppose you have—that this queer stunt,
Properly worked, could mean a lot of real
Red-hot Publicity !

[FAUST *shrugs negligently.*]

                     Fr'instance, you
Might meet this queer infernal pal of yours
Wearing my brand of boots ! It'd Go Big !
I'd see that it was boosted everywhere.
" BOOLS' BOOTS. THE SORT THAT SMART MEN
    WEAR, EVEN
TO MEET THE DEVIL IN ! "—something like that.
How does it strike you ? Hey ?
FAUST (*distastefully*) : No, thanks, you tout.

    [SIR HENRY, *accustomed to such rebuffs, merely
       waggles his red hands and looks appealingly
       at* LADY UNA, *who stares through him.*]

FAUST (*to* LADY UNA) :
This afternoon some idiot called to ask
What kind of pen I used the day I signed
My contract with—you know. Was it a Plonk,
Or was it one of Whibberley's Self-Fillers ?
He offered me a handsome sum. I had
Him thrown downstairs ; I fear quite violently.
I've also been approached to give a short
And pithy broadcast of my final speech.
Preceded by a chatty paper on
" What It Feels Like To Interview the Devil."
And yesterday the Cheery Magazine—— .

    [*The clock softly begins to chime midnight.
       Before the second stroke the door opens, and a
       tall, sardonic figure, flashily dressed (see
       "Enoch Soames," by Max Beerbohm), stands*

5   65

*on the threshold in a rather overdone melo-
dramatic attitude.*]

THE STRANGER (*using the old formula*) :
Hither to me !

[LADY UNA *grinds her cigarette-end into an
ash-tray and languidly puts up a lorgnette.
SIR HENRY BOOLS' little eyes are bulging.
FAUST, pale but composed, squares his
shoulders.*]

FAUST (*breaking a tense silence*) :
Certainly. . . . . Have a drink ?

[*The time is* 1.45. *The room now holds only
two people—*LADY UNA DASH *and the tall
STRANGER.*]

LADY UNA (*languidly*) : Really ?
THE STRANGER :   I do assure you !
LADY UNA :   Don't you know,
I think you're rather int'resting ! You *swear*
Never to worry Freddy any more ?

[*The* STRANGER *hesitates, but is lost. He is in
the hands (but doesn't know it) of the most
expert siren in London. After a slight shrug
he nods.*]

LADY UNA (*sighing gently*) :
How splendid. Now you'd better ring the bell.
It's late. I must go on.
THE STRANGER (*hoarsely—poor devil !*) :
And—may I call ?
LADY UNA :
To-morrow. I am in from three to five.
I think you may have tea with me. My friends
Will simply love to meet you. Now, please.

TWELVE OF THE CLOCK

[*He rings and helps her on with her cloak.
She goes out. The tall* STRANGER *sinks back
dazed on the divan.*]

THE STRANGER (*realising he is vanquished*) :

Hell !

[EXPLICIT]

Ballade of Spring and Mrs. Bossom

" Solvitur acris hiems," etc.
—Hor. Carm. I, 4.

Spring's silver trumpets shrilly blow,
The linkèd panthers, swart and lean,
Drawing the Wine-God's chariot go ;
The laughing Mænads prink and preen ;
Drunk with the blushful Hippocrene
A shouting wind conveys the news
To Satyrs prancing through the green . . .
But Mrs. Bossom will refuse.

Euoe ! With a maniac glow
The god's red eyes survey the scene ;
Silenus nid-nods to and fro,
Bland as a vine-wreathed Rural Dean ;
Whom is he beckoning ? Miss Bean ?
Or is it Mrs. Henry Tooze ?
How sad ! How *really* sad, I mean !—
But Mrs. Bossom will refuse.

Where are the girls we used to know ?
The wearers of the bombazine ?
Miss Splurge and Mrs. Boldero,
And awful Lady Gabbadine ?
They would have scorned to reign as Queen
O'er goats, and men with hoofs for shoes !
You say Miss Stinger once was seen. . . .?
But Mrs. Bossom will refuse !

68

SPRING AND MRS. BOSSOM

ENVOI

Prince, in that Stygian demesne,
When Charon rows across the ooze,
His disappointment will be keen—
But Mrs. Bossom will refuse.

Pastoral ∽ ∽ ∽ ∽ ∽

THE Pastoral which follows is founded on, and may be played in conjunction with, Beethoven's Pastoral Symphony, No. VI, Op. 68. This Symphony is divided by Beethoven into five parts :

1º *Allegro ma non troppo* : Joyous impressions on arrival in the country.
2º *Andante molto moto, quasi allegretto* : Scene on the banks of a stream.
3º *Allegro* : Merry gathering of peasants.
4º *Allegro* : Thunderstorm.
5º *Allegretto* : Shepherds' song, and thanks-- giving to rural deity after storm.

It has been necessary to revise the descriptions of the second, third, fourth, and fifth movements slightly in order to adapt Beethoven's impressions more closely to English rural conditions.

Now we can get on, I think.

A RURAL LANDSCAPE, WITH A VILLAGE

I.—*Allegro ma non troppo*

Two RUSTICKS *cross the scene. A* TRAVELLER *appears from the opposite side.*

THE TRAVELLER :
  Rusticks, well met ! The agricultural gods
  Look kindly on you !
FIRST RUSTICK : And you.
THE TRAVELLER : Thank ye, clods.

[The RUSTICKS *go out.]*

70

PASTORAL

THE TRAVELLER:

In scenes like this, where peaceful pleasures
   spring,
Tityrus, pride of Mantuan swains, might sing,
While nimble shepherds capered at their play,
And old *Damœtas* raised the tuneful lay ;
Ye heav'nly Nine, and thou, Pomona fair,
With fruit and various dessert in thy hair,
You, sunburnt *Faunus*, and blest *Ceres* too—
In fact, the usual agricultural crew—
Attend, and show a leg ! I celebrate
The pious pleasures of the rural state,
The joys of him who, far from civick strife,
Flies to the solace of a country life.

   [*A motor chaff-cutter backfires loudly.*]

Encompassed round with cows and lambs and
   churns,
With mild but strong Benevolence he burns,
Alike to gilded Pomp and Pride a foe,
His only joy to shake a careless toe
With merry rusticks in the rural dance,
To pluck a simple posy, or, perchance,
Reclining on some flowery bank at ease,
To stand some lovely village maid a cheese ;
To pore with fervour on some purling stream,
Or, while his orbs with hopeless rapture beam,
To wander lonely in some darkling grove,
While all the woods resound with vows of Love !

   [*Two more* RUSTICKS *cross the scene.*]

How happy he who thus, remote from fears,
Himself to all the rustick throng endears,
His daily sport to dally with the fair,
And twine the tangles of *Næera's* hair.

   [*He speaks to the* RUSTICKS.]

71

Where is the garage, rurals ?

[*They point in dumb-show.*]

Thank ye, louts.

But revellers approach ; I hear their shouts.

[*He goes out dancing.*]

II.—*Andante molto moto, quasi allegretto.*

[*A rout of* MECHANICKS *enter and dance round
the village Petrol-Pump. On their dispersal
the* TRAVELLER *re-enters.*]

THE TRAVELLER :

Sweet Slugwash, loveliest village of the plain,
Long may destruction threaten thee in vain !
Blest refuge of my soul, which year by year
Dost ever grow more lovely and more dear,
Whether a new tin garage cheers the eye,
Or signs for petrol animate the sky,
Or new red villas, or great stacks of coal,
Refresh the mind and harmonise the whole,
Or whether, swiftly raised by eager hands,
Ye Olde Elizabethanne Tea-Shoppe stands,
Or whether Business Men their paunches stuff
In what was once the George, on Slugwash
  Rough,
And fiercely agitate the urgent bell
Bawling for cocktails in the new Hotel—
Fondly to thee I turn, beloved vill.,
Curst be the hand that e'er could do thee ill !

[*Overcome with these sentiments, the* TRAVELLER
*rests his head in his hands during the next
two movements.*]

III.—*Allegro.*

A gathering of RUSTICKS, *grousing bitterly about
the fine weather.*

72

PASTORAL

IV.—*Allegro.*

A Thunderstorm; after which a gathering of
RUSTICKS, *grousing angrily about the rain.*

V.—*Allegretto, quasi giocoso.*

A gathering of RUSTICKS, *grousing morosely about
everything. To them, from the opposite side,
enters a* STRANGER, *briskly.*

THE STRANGER:
Why oafs, what mien is this ?   Why do my ears
Receive no meed of rude and raucous cheers ?
What secret griefs perturb your stockish minds ?
FIRST RUSTICK:
Be you the gent from Lunnon ?
THE STRANGER: Truly, hinds.
Forbear to clog your lumpish wits with woe,
For ever Reason was to Grief a foe,
Shall we not bid the Fancy fondly stray,
Where Piety and Duty point the way ?

> [*He unrolls a Great Plan, at which the* RUSTICKS
> *gather round, giving vent to uncouth appro-
> bation.*]

THE TRAVELLER:
Earthworms, forbear to grizzle ; for it seems
Truth from this Stranger's orbs doth fling his
beams.
> [*He speaks to the* STRANGER.]

I bid you welcome, sir, and fain would know
What agitates these lumps of subsoil.

THE STRANGER: So !

> [*The* STRANGER *comes forward and addresses
> the* TRAVELLER.]

73

ON STRAW

On Mincio's banks, in bounteous *Cæsar's*
   reign,
They deemed the Golden Age had come again,
And *Vergil* painted with his brightest strokes
The lives and works of agricultural blokes ;
So now the Golden Age returns, for here,
In this blest village, shortly will appear
A fine Glue-Factory ! A huge Sheet-Iron Mill !
Two more new Garages ! On yonder hill
A splendid Foundry, skirting Slugwash Pond !
A hundred villas in the vale beyond !
And, in yon winding honeysuckled lane,
A simply gorgeous House for the Insane !

> [*At this the* RUSTICKS *give three roaring cheers
> and break into a merry dance, while the*
> STRANGER *contemplates them with benevo-
> lence and the* TRAVELLER *reverently removes
> his hat ; and so to the*

FINALE]

Note : In addition to the orchestral instruments
provided for in Beethoven's score, the following
may for the purposes of the Pastoral be added,
if desired, for the last movement and Finale :

> One F sharp steam whistle,
> One sheet of iron, with bang bars,
> One B-sharp motor exhaust,
> Three B-flat saxophones,
> Six rattles,
> Three American high-blast motor ploughs,
> Twelve typewriters, and
> Three dynamos.

The enormous orchestral value of the type-
writer, I need hardly remind musicians, has been
amply demonstrated by the late Erik Satie, and

those of most of the other instruments by such masters as Strauss, Honegger, and American jazz composers.

The Pastoral is dedicated to Henry Bessemer, inventor of the Blast Furnace.

Of Fairies

Q. GOOD evening. Do you believe in Faries ?
A. Yes.

Q. Would you mind giving me your reason ?
A. *Mordious!* I can give you one hundred and nine reasons ! The first is that the following leaders of Modern Thought—

Mr. Henry Ford,	Mr. Sidney Webb,
Professor Freud,	Mr. Jacob Epstein,
Dean Inge,	Mr. H. G. Wells,

—do not believe in Fairies. Hence we have at the very start, as you see, a strong *prima-facie* case for assuming that Fairies exist.

Q. You have never actually seen a Fairy ?
A. What of that ? I have never actually seen the Lord Mayor.

Q. Do you know where any Fairies are to be found ?
A. I think there are hardly any in England. It is well known (and there is a charming and ancient poem explaining it) that most of the Fairies vanished from our dear English lanes at the same time as the Friars ; that would be about the year 1539, the thirtieth of Henry VIII, who suffered so damnably from boils. The Industrial Revolution of the early nineteenth century decimated the lean remainder. They tell me that nowadays a few Fairies, the last survivors, are still to be found up and down England—one or two in Devon, and another near the iron-foundry at

Peacehaven (on the Sussex Downs) and another in Huddersfield. In the Celtic countries there are more, but they rarely show themselves since the Celtic Renaissance.

[*A Pause.*]

Q. I see you include a Mr. Sidney Webb in your list. Is he *the* Webb ?

A. Most certainly.

Q. Forgive my appearing to question your familiarity with the minds of the Great, but how do you know Mr. Webb (for instance) does not believe in Fairies ?

A. Since you mention it, I confess I only stuck him in to give the list an appearance of weight. *I personally think he does believe.* And more.

Q. What do you mean ?

A. Zookers ! Flidderkins ! *Par le sambreguoy de bois !* I mean that it is highly probable that Mr. Webb not only believes in Fairies, but is one.

Q. Bah ! Pooh !

A. I am certain of it. Would you like it proved ? I might prove it you in any one of the thirty-one magical ways which Her Trippa the necromancer suggested to Panurge : that is, by

Aeromancy,	Giromancy,
Alectryomancy,	Hydromancy,
Alentomancy,	Icthyomancy,
Alphitomancy,	Leconomancy,
Anthropomancy,	Libanomancy,
Astragalomancy,	Negromancy,
Axionomancy,	Onomatomancy,
Botomancy,	Onymancy,
Capnomancy,	Pyromancy,
Catopromancy,	Sciomancy,
Cephalomancy,	Sicomancy,
Ceromancy,	Sternomancy,

Cheromomancy,	Stichomancy
Choiramancy,	Tephromancy, or
Coscinomancy,	Tyromancy.
Gastromancy,	

But I will not do this, because (firstly) it would require certain rare accessories, such as a Brehèmont Cheese, a quantity of frankincense, a crystal globe, a brazier of burning charcoal, a boiling Ass's Head, fair water, some wax, a sieve, a hog's-bladder, and wood-ashes ; as also a black Cock, a Pentagon, the Green Stone called *Xaxaxthamoun*, and other cabbalistic properties prescribed by the Grand Grimoire and the Black Book of Thélème ; and (secondly) because the practice of such vile arts is rightly forbidden Christian men by at least five Œcumenical Councils (not counting Ephesus and Trent), and also by the Bull *Quemadmodum plurimi*. Therefore, I will not so much as touch this foul diabolical stuff, but will prove it instead by Logic : I mean the only kind of Logic worth a hoot, that is, Scholastic Logic.

Q. Oh !

A. Yes, it may hurt ; for we are not used to reasoning with our minds, but rather through our bowler hats. On this account we will not employ the formal mode, with *ad primum*, and *praeterea*, and *sed contra*, and *respondeo*. The Angelic Doctor uses it, but it is death to a jazz-nourished mind. Therefore we——

Q. I do not like these Swedish matches.

A. No ?

Q. Always going out and so forth.

A. Yes ? We will merely argue it informally and in a non-technical manner. We begin with this statement :—

It seems that Mr. Webb is not a Fairy.

78

You see we are first assuming the contrary of what we want to prove. Let us proceed to consider the distinguishing marks of a Fairy. A Fairy (for example) has silvery laughter and slides down rainbows. Has Mr. Webb either of these marks? No? Then Mr Webb is not a Fairy. A Fairy is diaphanous, airy, tricksy, neat, gay, slim, dainty, and swift. Therefore Mr. Webb is not a Fairy. Again, Fairies do not draw up with delight arid schemes for the stricter strait-jacketing and dragooning of the universe, nor carry umbrellas, nor wear pince-nez, nor scrabble and peck in the horrid dust-hole of Economics. Therefore Mr. Webb is not a Fairy.

Q. No, indeed.

A. Wait.

Q. I beg your pardon.

A. We now proceed to the diet of Fairies, which is chiefly (as the poet Herrick reports) the horns of papery Butterflies, the Cuckoo's spittle, the pith of sugared Rush, fuzz-ball Puddings, the bag of Bees, the beards of Mice, the dewlaps of Snails, Nightingale's heart, and other foods rich in proteids. Whereas most Fabians (see Bossom : *Natural History of Battersea*, 1906) live on gritty Bath-Buns and lukewarm milk. Therefore Mr. Webb is not a F——.

Q. But——

A. You are going to say that some Fabians notoriously live an ants' eggs and dishwater! I agree. It is a very good *contra*. Vegetarians and Fairies have this in common. We will come to this in a moment. Pray stop that mewing noise. We now come to our *responsio*, or Respond, which is : It is clearly absurd to say that Mr. Webb is not a Fairy, since

(*a*) Though he is not actually known to dance on

moonbeams, it is evident from the lightsomeness and winsome grace of "*Some Observations on the Guffin Minority Report on Ca' Canny in the Iron and Slag Trade, 1889,*" that he could do so if he liked.

(*b*) A devotion to statistics is no proof that a man is not a Fairy. Many Chartered Accountants are Trolls ("*The C.A. Year Book, 1908*"). The Fairy Uk-Jee wore pince-nez (Mrs. Gallop, "*Thoughts on Free Trade,*" 1887). Leprechauns often carry rolled umbrellas in the City (Rubbage, "*Our Exports,*" 1912).

(*c*) A Vegetarian diet, though conducive to pimples, at the same time purifies the emotions and frees the aspirations (E. Miles, "*How I Tamed My Ganglions,*" 1922). Therefore, it is possible that some Vegetarians (and Fabians) are actually Fairies now, while others are becoming so. Similarly with Mr. Webb.

[*A Pause.*]

Q. (heartily) : Anyway, he was a fine swimmer in his day. That Niagara business—— But why do you kick your hat about so madly ?

A. It is yours. Get out !

A Defence of Bakers

" *LES Patrons Boulangers sont des commerçants égoistes, des exploiteurs féroces.*"—Opening sentence of a Poster issued recently by the Journeymen Bakers of Paris.

" *The Master Bakers are selfish money-grubbers and ferocious sweaters.*"

I. General Introduction, expressive of the horror and consternation of the Author at this rash declaration.

> What ! Is it true that Bakers can
> Oppress or bully any man ?

Ship at Sea, hastily carrying outraged English Master Baker home after 1 hour in France.	Master Baker's bake-house at 6 o'clock on a still Thursday m o r n i n g i n February	Defunct M a s t e r B a k e r winging his way through celestial æther.

II. Continuation of the Foregoing ; followed by a Reasoned Defence of Bakers and a Brief Survey of their Virtues.

> It makes my heart go sick and ache
> To hear such things of men who bake !

ON STRAW

The Baker's soul is white as snow,
And as he mildly slaps his dough
Some portions to his face adhere . . .
But does he rage and swell ?   No Fear !
Remarking that it looks like rain
He simply wipes it off again.

Revered alike by man and beast
The Baker rises with the yeast ;
He nothing common does, or mean,
Upon this memorable scene,
But at a very early hour
He flings himself upon the flour.

III. *Parenthetic Reflection on this.*

At 3 a.m. he leaves his bed.
I'd rather—Oh ! My Hat !—be dead.

IV. *Resumption of Panegyric.*

Behold the Baker, with a shout,
Dashing the cereal stuff about ;
If some should fall upon the floor
He simply scoops a spadeful more,
Knowing that when he sweeps it up
He stands to win a Wholemeal Cup,
And everything will be just so
Ut erat in principio.
Behold him seize the water-can
And gently rallying his man
With piety and ardour blent,
Sprinkle the friendly element !
What verve !   What manly cheerfulness !
What *joie de vivre* !   Gosh !   What a mess !

A DEFENCE OF BAKERS

Gargling Mixture used by Bakers' Wives before singing "Thora."

Negro Master Baker baking black bread at midnight.

Bird's-eye view from the Matterhorn of Master Baker removing dough from his ears with a rubber sponge.

V. *Meditation on the Domestic Happiness of Bakers.*

The Baker is entirely free
From dark and latent savagery ;
Or else, at least, he takes it out
By pounding slabs of dough about,
And thus—so queer a thing is Life—
He never needs to thump his wife,
Who thus is not inclined to rove
And dresses, as a rule, in mauve.

VI. *Continuation of Main Thesis.*

But see ! Amorphous, vast, and still,
Subservient to the Baker's will,
And quivering at his slightest frown,
The dough lies where he flung it down !
But not, observe, entirely in
Its trough, receptacle, or bin.
For part (as we have seen) adheres
Not only to the Baker's ears
But, seeing it is always sticky,
To eyebrows, whiskers, neck, and dickey,
And at the end of every bout
Whitens the Baker's massive snout ;

83

Making him thus, from toes to scalp,
More lovely than a snow-clad Alp.

VII. (a) *Note on the Ritual Significance of
White.*

" *Albo colore utitur* . . ."
So runs the Rubric ; we infer
That White means Happiness, and hence
Purity, Peace, and Innocence.

(b) *Expression of Nonchalance concerning Bakers
in East Africa, Liberia, Jamaica, etc.*

Under a tropic sun, alack !
The Baker frequently goes black ;
Can Virtue veil herself in soot ?
I do not care a single hoot.

VIII. *Resumption of Argument.*

We cannot now consider the
Minutiæ of the industry—
The way the dough is punched and rolled
By men directed and controlled
With consummate address and tact
Under the Baking (Powers) Act ;
But anyhow, it may be said,
They turn it somehow into bread.

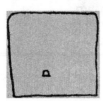

Entrance to Cockroach Ranch.

Fragment of Plainsong intoned by Cockroach after safe escape from apoplectic Master Baker.

Egg laid by Nightingale shortly after being praised in Verse by the poet Keats.

A DEFENCE OF BAKERS

IX. Parenthetic but Spirited Challenge by the Author to Amateur Literary Men.

My bread, it seems, you try to snatch
From out my mouth? Come, then! Despatch!
It leaves me cool and calm enough—
I very rarely eat the stuff.

X. Final Pæan.

In dazzling white the Baker stands,
Are those (though over-large) the hands
That could—an action to deplore—
Imbrue themselves in Infant Gore?
Can boots like those no mercy own
But wade through bloodshed to a throne?
Do burning villages attest
The ravening Baker's frantic zest?
Or does he sweep athwart the plain,
The aged widow's scourge and bane,
And, while her peaceful home he wrecks,
Trample on fainting maidens' necks?
No! It is false! It is a lie
That Bakers are habitually
Prone to such cursed uncivil tricks!
Enough for them to pat and mix
The yielding dough, to chase the spare
But hardy cockroach to his lair,
To lend more brightness to the bun,
To mould the shapely Sally Lunn . . .
And finally, without surprise,
To cleave the glowing liquid skies—
Complacent, smug, aloof, entire,
Attended by an Angel Quire—
And vanish in the blinding blue.

ON STRAW

For what is Beautiful is True,
So Keats (or someone)[1] says, one gleans.

You must not ask me what it means.

[1] I fancy Mrs. Henry Wood
Said " What is Beautiful is Good."

Nine Cantankerous Fables ✄ ✄ ✄

THE OLD MAN AND HIS SONS

AN Old Man desiring to Inflict a Moral Lesson on his Sons, who were perpetually Quarrelling, took a Quantity of Sticks and, Tying them in a Bundle, invited Each of his Sons to Break the Bundle. This they were Unable to Do.. Then, cutting the String and Handing them each a Separate Stick, the Old Man (with a Fatuous Smile) desired his Sons to Try Again. They all Succeeded in Breaking the Sticks Singly except the Youngest Son, who, Profiting by his Aged Parent's Absorption in what he (Rightly, or Wrongly) Considered a Futile and Boring Trick, had Seized the Opportunity of Rifling the Old Man's Chest and Getting Away with the Money-Bags.

Moral.—Unity is Strength, but in Big Business you need Initiative and the Power of making Quick Decisions.

THE MAN AND HIS GOOSE

A Man had a Goose which Laid Every Day an Egg of the Purest Gold. One Day this Man, who had been Reading the Works of Ricardo, Adam Smith, John Stuart Mill, and other Economic Bores, stood for a Time in Silence, Contemplating his Goose. He then Said to Himself, " It Seems

87

Probable that this Goose, which Yields me at Present One Golden Egg per Day, should Contain in its Interior such a Reserve of Capital of the Precious Metal as would Make my Killing and Opening Her a Sound Economic Proposition." So saying the Man took an Axe and Beat the Auriferous Fowl very Soundly about the Mazzard until it Gave up the Ghost; after which, Rummaging Carefully in its Inside, the Man found, as he had Anticipated (and as, Indeed, was the Only Logical Conclusion, considering its Behaviour), Large Quantities of Gold in place of Giblets and What Not. Taking this Gold, the Man soon Acquired a Vast Fortune and, entering Politics and Bribing too Lavishly on the Opposition Side, was Ultimately Assassinated by Hired Bravoes in the Pay of the Prime Minister.

Moral.—There is always a Catch in it.

THE BULL, THE LIONESS, AND THE HUNTER

A Bull finding a Lion-Cub asleep seized the Opportunity to Gore it to Death; on which the Lioness, coming up, Began to Lament Bitterly the Decease of her Offspring. A Hunter seeing her Distress stood a Little Way off and said to her, " Think how Many there Are who have Reason to Lament the Loss of their Offspring, whose Deaths have been Caused by You ! "
As he spoke Thus a Large Baulk of Wood fell from a Tree and Completely Annihilated him.

Moral.—The sudden End of a Prig is Always Attractive.

88

CUPID AND DEATH

The little god Cupid, being Tired of Play, ran into the Cave of Death to Rest, Flinging his Quiver on the Ground; and on Waking and Gathering up his Scattered Arrows he ran out again Without Perceiving that Many of them had become inextricably Mixed with the Arrows of Death. Thus it is that many Quite Young People Die and some Quite Oldish People get a Still Worse Time.

Moral.—Without some Sort of System no Business can be Run without Annoying Mistakes.

THE DOGS AND THE FOX

A number of Dogs, finding one Day the Skin of a Lion, began to Tear it to Pieces with their Teeth. A Fox, passing and Seeing them, said, " If this Lion were Alive, you would Soon Find Out that his Claws were Stronger than Your Teeth."

A Publisher, happening Also to Pass that way and hearing these Words, was Greatly Impressed with their Truth and Wisdom, and Offered the Fox Large Sums for the Privilege of Publishing them in a Limited Edition on Vellum, each Copy Numbered and Signed by the Author. In Consequence of this the Fox became a Figure in Literary Circles and one of the Worst Bores in London.

Moral.—It is No Use emitting Bromides unless you can Capitalise them, like Mr. ——.

THE FALCONER AND THE PARTRIDGE

A Partridge being Caught in a Falconer's Net offered to Decoy other Partridges into the same Predicament if the Falconer would Only Let him Go Free. At this the Good Falconer Waxed Very Angry and exclaimed, " What ! Are you Fallen so Low as to Sacrifice your Friends to Save Yourself ? " He then remained Silent for Some Time, Chewing his Whiskers in Abhorrence and Moral Indignation ; and Finally, turning to the Treacherous Bird, he added, in a Manly and Resonant Voice, " Anyhow, You Will Have, while Thus Engaged, to Find your Own Food, and we will Have It So in the Contract."

Moral.—Inattention to Detail has Wrecked Many a Promising Deal.

THE SPORTSMAN AND THE DOVE

A Sportsman going into the Woods one Day observed a Dove in a Tree, and Raising his Gun to his Shoulder prepared to Take Aim. But as he Did So a Snake in the Grass, on which he had Inadvertently Trodden, Up and Bit him in the Ankle ; at which, Greatly Mortified, the Sportsman Gave Vent to this Exclamation : " Fate has brought Destruction on. me as I was Contriving the Destruction of Another."

Moral.—When going into the City it is as Well to Wear Spats, or you may be Frightfully Stung.

NINE CANTANKEROUS FABLES

THE EAGLE AND HIS CAPTOR

A Man having Captured an Eagle immediately Clipped its Wings and Placed in on his Poultry Farm, where it was Much Exposed to Cutting Comments from Several Hens. A Poor but Kindly Neighbour Purchased the Eagle and Allowed its Feathers to Grow, whereupon the Grateful Bird, after Taking a Trial Spin, returned with a Hare, which it Presented to its Benefactor. At this a Fox standing by said, " Surely you should Propitiate not This Man but Your Former Owner, who may Catch You and Clip your Wings Again ! "

The Eagle, with a Slight Wink, replied, " Do not Fuss Yourself, Henry. I have already Pleased the Other Bloke with a Gift of several Hens, formerly the Property of Kind-Hearted William ; who (I may Add) will Inevitably Blame it on You."

Moral.—While one should Endeavour to be Polite, it is as Well to be Polite to the Rich *first of all.*

THE OX, THE BEE, THE LION, THE ELEPHANT
THE ANT, THE DOG, THE CRANE, THE WOMBAT
AND THE OLD MAN

An Ox, a Bee, a Lion, an Elephant, an Ant, a Dog, a Crane, and a Wombat were Assembled one Day in the Woods, Giving Tongue in Turn to Any Amount of Practical Wisdom and Improving Conversation. Seeing an Old Man approaching, the Animals Determined to Elect him Judge of their Efforts. After Some Hours of Hard Mental

Concentration they Demanded the Name of the Winner, only to Find, to their Extreme Chagrin, that the Old Man was as Deaf as a Newt and Had not Heard a Single Word. They thereupon Set On the Aged Person and Bit him so Severely that his Boots were Full of Blood.

Moral.—It is No Use Putting Over a Good Line until you are Sure of your Market.

Of Pleasant Noises ✑   ✑   ✑   ✑

ABOUT the end of the fourteenth century there
lived in the grassy Norman valley called the
Vaux de Vire, on the edge of the Cotentin, a fulling-
miller named Olivier Basselin, whose nose was
ruddier than the cherry, whose laugh could be
heard on a clear day as far away as St. Lô, and
who wrote some of the best drinking-songs in the
world ; of which I have a large number in a
book.

This roaring miller was the chief of a little band,
cluster, or gaggle of country poets, nearly all
peasants ; for if the Norman, according to Octave
Mirabeau and Maupassant, is hard, avaricious,
gluttonous, and rooted to his soil (he also gave us
government and reopened for us islanders a window
on the rest of Europe, greatly to the annoyance
of a supercilious gentleman in a bowler hat with
whom I had an argument the other day) he could
once both make up and sing good songs. Now
among the songs of Olivier Basselin there is one
which he made one day on passing the village
cooper's and hearing him hammering at a
cask. It begins :

> *O tintamarre plaisant*
> *Et doulcement resonnant*
> *Des tonneaulx que l'on relie !*

" O the delicious sweetly-resounding racket of
wine-casks being coopered ! " And he continues :
" Faith, a sign that we shall be drinking soon !

By Gosh, the lovely clamour ! It has saved me from dying of melancholy this very day ! ".

Now Heaven and my Patron forbid that I should fall into the disgraceful error of praising a wine-bibber, and a medieval at that ! I dare say the same quick gush of joy informs a totally abstaining and modern breast on passing a cocoa factory and hearing the bean-polishers singing at their work ; and I dare say Mr. Eustace Miles feels the same on hearing the rattle of the nuts pouring into the Mock-Steak machine. *O tintamarre plaisant !* And this brings me to my point, namely, that there are thousands of noises so pleasant and gladsome, whether of themselves or through their associations, that they make the heart fly and twitter like a bird. Did not the clink of bottles please the infant Gargantua so that " at the sound of Pintes and Flaggons he would on a sudden fall into an Extasie, as if he had then tasted of the Joyes of Paradise " ? Hey ?

Another bibber, I fear. But not (please Heaven) medieval.

The war horse in Holy Writ loved the sound of the trumpet, and would say, Ha ! Trumpets are always a pleasant noise (provided they are not sounding you to rise early and combat) : and their brazen uproar is particularly heartening at a Coronation, or in the forest scene in " Boris Godounov," or even in that massy Requiem of Berlioz—though in this they put one in mind of Death : another medieval superstition.

The squeals of a bumptious critic threatened with the State punishment called *peine forte et dure,* now, alas ! abolished, I would walk a long way to hear ; at the same time lightly criticising the key and timbre of his yells.

The noise made by nightingales in the full

moon has been commented on at enormous length by a mort of poets.

> *How thick the bursts come crowding through the leaves !*
> *Again—thou hearest !*
> *Eternal Passion !*
> *Eternal Pain !*

That was written by an Inspector of. Schools under the Government of Queen Victoria. The noise of water boiling in a kettle, the noise of a great wood thrashed by a storm, the noise of bees bumbling in a summer afternoon, of horses galloping, of a fiddle playing Couperin, of ducks quacking on green English ponds, of little waves guggling round a boat's bows, of strong masterful men utterly discomfited, of bacon sputtering in a pan in the cool of the morning, of knaves foaming against Providence, of bells heard at sea, of adulterators of honest liquor unmasked and objurgating, of—

Shall I tell you, by the way, what the old French poet said in a Ballade about this last kind of scoundrel ? He said: " May the swabs have their giblets tickled with a Turkish arrow and a sharp sword ; may Greek fire scorch their thatch and a great tempest scatter their brains ; may their carrion bodies hang from a high gibbet, and may they die very swiftly in agony from the gout ; I demand and request also that they be prodded with red-hot iron bars and flayed alive by ten hangmen, boiled in oil in the morning, and torn apart by four ramping great horses—the taverners who hocus our good wine." I call that a Wish. There are two more stanzas like that.

—of girls laughing on an April day, of the crackling and whispering of a beech-log fire in

February, of a hunting-horn heard in the green
depths of the forest (though one poet I know
esteems this a melancholy noise), of Andalusian
voices lisping at nightfall, of drums throbbing far
off to the tramp of infantry, of groaning farm-
wagons heavy with harvest, of stockbrokers
howling after a market crash, of ice tinkling in a
jug under the Dog-Star, of grasshoppers chirping
in August hayfields, of high tides swishing regu-
larly on shingle beaches, of distant scythes being
honed, of anchor-chains rattling down in haven :
all these are lovely and pleasant noises, enlarging
and uplifting human hearts.

I would add, also, the bawling of Mr. * * * *,
a Leading Thinker, when menaced with punishment by the State for endeavouring to befuddle
and incornifistigropilibustulate honest men's minds.
I would not have him dealt with in the stern old
way, that is by

(*a*) The Question Ordinary.

(*b*) The Boot, the favourite pastime of James
the First, whom the Scots gave us : a great
booby and dribbler, and half-mad even by
Northern standards.

(*c*) The punishment awarded Gossouin de Louet,
a citizen of Paris, in the year 1435, for plotting
to throw the English out of Paris ; he was
*par gehine et question tresdurement traveillié
de son corps*, which is something most uncomfortable, but was pardoned by Bedford,
acting for Henry VI. I have just been
reading his case.

These were punishments for men. I would
have the Leading Thinker merely slapped and

exposed to the derision of all true citizens. His screams, I think, would be in the Mixo-Lydian Mode, on the dominant F sharp : a very pleasing noise.

There is one noise, a Master Noise, which to some may be hackneyed, to others harsh, to others' meaningless, to others dull, to others tuneless, but to me exquisite, soothing, rare, and never-too-often-to-be-repeated : the noise (forgive my quaint frenzy) of great fat cheques being ripped violently from their moorings and presented unawares to poor men. Match me (as the Don sang, but referring to a rose-red city of the East)—

Match me such marvel, whether East or West,
So full of blooming ecstasy and zest.

I have done.

The Tanker Affair ∽ ∽ ∽ ∽

AS I was sitting alone in an armchair the other afternoon, composing a bitter letter to a laundry on the subject of Socks, and simultaneously endeavouring in my mind to turn into English a rondeau of Christine de Pisan, a visitor was announced, and J. F. Guffin, the poet, walked in. He was flushed and stood on one leg and coughed. I asked him the reason for this awkwardness. He said he had been feeling awkward ever since he killed W. P. Tanker.

He said, blushing furiously, " I can't help it. It is stupid of me to feel like this. I killed him last Tuesday."

Let us pause a moment and survey the general situation. J. F. Guffin and W. P. Tanker both belong to the Wheeble Group. Anyone who knows anything of London's literary coteries and cliques knows that the Wheeble Group is one of the most exclusive and powerful. Its members are O. H. J. Wheeble himself, W. P. Tanker, J. F. Guffin, Little Bilberry, F. R. G. Loofah, and a few others of literary importance. Each member of the group has his week in the *Sarcophagus*, that influential critical review. One week, for example, one finds on an important page :

O. H. J. WHEEBLE
By W. P. Tanker

The next week one finds

LOOFAH—THE MAN
By George Bilberry

THE TANKER AFFAIR

And the next

THE ART OF J. F. GUFFIN
By O. H. J. Wheeble

And the next

W. P. TANKER, POET, CRITIC, AND HUMANIST
A Survey and an Appreciation
By F. R. G. Loofah

And so on, each in his turn. Do no confuse them with the Punting Group, which includes Wryly Punting, R. P. Bawl, Timperley, Striver, J. H. H. Gudgeon, and others. The Wheebles hate the Puntings like poison. It is said that Wheeble met Punting the other day on top of a No. XI omnibus in the Strand and gave him a simply awful look. It is necessary to be quite clear about all this. Bilberry admires Wheeble and Wheeble admires Bilberry; Bawl thinks Gudgeon the greatest man in England, and Gudgeon says publicly that Bawl is wonderful, quite wonderful. As Euclid would put it, they are marvellous each to each, but to their opposite angles just like hell.

To return to J. F. Guffin. He stood there, obviously embarrassed, saying something about its being a ridiculous position.

I said: "I heard you had killed Tanker. Somebody or other told me on Thursday—or it might have been Friday."

J. F. Guffin fidgeted.

"I did it on Tuesday afternoon."

"Why?"

"Oh, I don't know," said J. F. Guffin impatiently. "Anyway, Wheeble is letting me write the appreciation of Tanker in next week's *Sarcophagus* instead of Bilberry. What I want you to

99

tell me is the name of something to cure this infernal blushing and self-consciousness. Whenever I go into a room fools stare and whisper: 'Look! There's Guffin, who killed Tanker!' I go red to the roots of my hair. Makes me feel such an ass."

" What did you do it with ? "

" I hit him with the bronze head of Wheeble by Popstein—it was on the mantelpiece, you know. Loofah's made an epigram about it."

" I don't see," I said at length, " why you should come to me. I don't much care about being mixed up in this rather undignified business. What does Wheeble say ? "

" Wheeble," replied J. F. Guffin simply, " hasn't spoken to any of us since the Duchess of Rye's reception."

" Did the newspapers make any comment ? "

J. F. Guffin produced a cutting. It read:

" SCENE " IN FLEET-STREET OFFICE

WELL-KNOWN POET KILLED BY COLLEAGUE

AMUSING INCIDENT

The offices of the *Sarcophagus*, the well-known critical review, were the scene this afternoon of a curious incident, Mr. J. F. Guffin, the poet and assistant editor, murdering Mr. W. P. Tanker, the poet and critic.

Interviewed after the incident, Mr. Guffin declined to make any statement. " It is a purely private matter," he said.

" Had you not a great admiration for the deceased ? " Mr. Guffin was asked.

" Certainly. We admired each other more, if possible, than any other two or three members of the group."

Mr. Guffin then referred to the new volume of poems he is publishing shortly, adding laughingly, " Tanker was to have written a warm appreciation. It is unfortunate that he should have been done in beforehand."

I handed the cutting back.
" Anything else ? "
" A symposium in *The Little Weekly*."
The general heading, I noted, was : " WHAT THEY THINK," and it began :

MR. ISIDORE POPSTEIN, THE FAMOUS SCULPTOR : I regard the affair as a gratifying tribute to Art. My portrait bust of Mr. Wheeble, with which the deed was carried out, was one of my finest bronzes. In it I had striven to interpret not merely the impact on a sublimated *ego* of a consciousness partially . . .

There was a great deal of that. I turned over.

MR. BURNETT SHAWLS : It is characteristic of the mental condition of the self-styled thinking minority that my time should be wasted by a demand of this sort. I am not concerned with the commonplace aspect of this affair. One literary critic more or less does not make any difference. Year in and year out I have been trying to hammer into the thick heads of this nation the obvious truth that criticism, whether literary or artistic. . . . .

There was a deal of that, too. I passed on.

The Editor of the *Tailor and Cutter* : The victim wore a blue dusted-effect D.B. lounge suit, with a shot herring-bone stripe, cut without distinction and entirely lacking in expression. The trousers were baggy and the cuff bore only two buttons, instead of three. The motive for this murder seems obvious.

ON STRAW

Mr. Eustace Smiles: The importance of deep breathing and rational diet is amply illustrated by this incident. Addiction to flesh-foods inevitably promotes turgid thinking and—if the present may be styled so—hasty action. In my pamphlet (No. 987, " Give Your Corpuscules a Chance ! ") I . . .

There was an awful lot of that. I passed over Miss Pearl Bright (who sketched the salient features of her career and thought Publicity had come to stay), the Lord Mayor, who said—

There are ideals in private, as in civic life. As the civic head of the Mother-City of Empire I cannot but think that to murder a gentleman of the literary eminence of Mr. Tanker is a step in the wrong direction. Our motto should be Service, not Self.

—Mr. Jack Bumpsey, the Chief Rabbi, the head waiter at the Saveloy, the Siamese Ambassador, Miss Gloria Snooper, Dean Ping, Mr. Steve Wonafughue, and of course Mr. Egbert Frankleigh. I yawned.

" Well ? " said J. F. Guffin.

" I think," I said judicially, " you are making too much of this incident. It isn't as if you had attacked a human being... I mean," I said with a vague gesture, " well—*is* it ? "

He did a most peculiar thing. He leaned over me and said in a low voice : " *Tee-hee-ee.*"

" What ? " I said, starting up.

" Your tea, sir."

I sat up, rubbing my eyes, and perceived that

his features had altered, that he wore club uniform and brass buttons, and that his eyes had become the eyes of a human man.

" Thank you, William," I said gratefully, taking a muffin.

Ballade of Death, Depression, and Shropshire ∽ ∽ ∽ ∽ ∽

On Wenlock Edge the clammy loam—
Eighty per cent blue clay, perhaps—
Provides a last long soggy home
For fine upstanding Shropshire chaps ;
The friends who knifed them (hence the gaps)
Have swung in Shrewsbury Gaol, egad !
Fate deals them the most frightful slaps. . . .
I'd hate to be a Shropshire Lad.

When Bredon men feel urged to roam
(The place is marked in Ordnance Maps)
They go all woozy in the dome,
Their girls recline in others' laps ;
The sun beats on their Lancer caps,
Their brains begin to boil like mad
And then the kindly bullet taps . . .
I'd hate to be a Shropshire Lad.

In Frant, Fazackerley, and Frome
The natives give each other raps,
Regular as a metronome
On wives in Wookey fall the straps ;
But rarely does a week elapse
Ere some Salopian, black and bad,
Stabs Dick, or Fred, and packs his traps—
I'd hate to be a Shropshire Lad.

DEATH, DEPRESSION, AND SHROPSHIRE

ENVOI

Prince, when the jolly little Japs
Slit themselves up, it makes you sad ;
What if the Shropshire drink' were Schnapps ?
I'd *hate* to be a Shropshire Lad.

In Praise of Plain Men ∽ ∽ ∽

THE year is 1785, and the scene a room in Windsor Castle. A tall footman, we may suppose, has just lighted the candles in the silver sconces and removed the tea equipage, and the curtains are drawn across the windows looking out across the Great Park. The Queen's women-in-waiting are sitting at their needlework ; it is their hour off duty in that dreary Court of George III, and they cackle decorously. Is Mrs. Schwellenberg there, the bullying old German harridan ? I forget. Little Fanny Burney is there, however, invincibly cheerful in spite of the iron discipline of Windsor, which is soon to leave her a nervous wreck. Suddenly the door opens. There is a hurried rising and curtsying. The King enters, red-faced, stout, kind, fatherly, and dull. Fanny Burney describes the scene in her Diary. The King sits down by her and begins to discuss the theatre, complaining of the lack of " good modern comedies " and of the " extreme immorality " of most of the old ones.

"At last" (says Fanny) "he came to Shakespeare. ' Was there ever,' cried he, ' such stuff as great part of Shakespeare ? Only one must not say so ! But what think you—what ? Is there not sad stuff ? What ? What ? '

" ' Yes, indeed, I think so, sir ; though mixed with such excellences, that——'

" ' Oh ! ' cried he, laughing good-humouredly, ' I know it is not to be said ! But it's true. Only it's Shakespeare, and nobody dare abuse him.' "

IN PRAISE OF PLAIN MEN

His most religious and gracious Majesty mentioned a number of things he disliked in Shakespeare, finishing by laughing again and exclaiming, " But one should be stoned for saying so ! "   He was a good man, was Farmer George, with his honest round face and his perpetual " What ? What ? "   He did not understand very much ; but then the best of us are not so very wonderful. I take George the Third to be the best type in all ages of the Plain Man, to whose praise and glory I have determined to compose this panegyric.

God bless the Plain Man. I see him, conscientious and sedate, with a boiled sort of eye and a rather prominent nose, pursuing his way with rectitude and jibbing nervously at anything suspicious or nonsensical ; though he has a veneration for scientists. (And quite properly. What words they use ! *Par le splendeur Dex !* What words !)   We are accustomed to regard him as of our own time, but he is not.   He is of all time. Be sure that when the Athenians sat entranced at a new tragedy of Euripides there was a Plain Man in the midst of them saying (in Greek) that no doubt it was all very clever, and this highbrow stuff was all right in its way, but give him (the Plain Man) a good old rough-and-tumble Saturnian gambol and no frills.   There was a Plain Man at the Court of King René also when the poets of Provence sang so gloriously, to the music of lutes and viols, the flames and darts of love.   One may imagine the buzz of conversation that followed.

A COURTIER : That was very fine, was it not ?

THE PLAIN MAN : Yes.   Very fine. . . . Is there much more ?

THE COURTIER : The *trouvère* Ramon de Vézélay is about to sing a sequence of sixteen *canzones* reflecting on the superior raptures of philosophic love, after which——

THE PLAIN MAN (*dogged*) : I see . . . When do the tumblers come on ?

For to the best type of Plain Man poetry is Death. He likes things expressed in a Plain Manner with no Flim-Flams and Fantastic Fooleries. He guesses (for example) that such a statement as

Night's candles are burnt out, and jocund day
Stands tiptoe on the misty mountains' tops

conceals something concrete and sensible about the dawn. Then why (asks the Plain Man with irritation) not say it plainly ? For instance :

Sun rises at 4.40, sets 10.5.
(High water 9.15 at London Bridge.)

Facts ! Facts ! That is the cry. There was once an obscure poet who wrote four lines which some people pretend to rank among the loveliest in the English language :

From the lone shieling and the misty island
Mountains divide us, and the waste of seas,
But still the heart is strong, the blood is Highland,
And we in dreams behold the Hebrides.

On which a Plain Man (so I hear), having worried and puzzled out to some extent its meaning, dictated a letter to the poet—for he was, like so many Plain Men, a Business Man also—to this effect :

Tel. London Wall 0097.
Tel. Address " Globularly."
987, Threadneedle Street,
London, E.C.
Nov. 13, 19—
Your Ref. : Q/15/76/J.
Dear Sir,—Our attention has been called to a statement by you that you view the Hebrides by means of

dreams, though actually some distance away. May we suggest that Rich Blood is the secret of Sound Refreshing Sleep ?

Insomnia, Dreams, etc., are most often caused by Anæmia and Digestive Troubles. A simple and efficacious Remedy for this is

GOOBER'S GLOBULES

(They Make the Stomach Sing !)

a sample box of which we enclose, and remain,
Faithfully,

(For GOOBER PRODUCTS, LTD.)

JAS. J. GOOBER,

JJG/HF.   Managing Director.

P.S.—Has it ever occurred to you that your Gums may be screaming for Gum-Joy ? GARGLENE is like a Gale in the Mouth.

But there was no reply.

O Plain Men ! O my brothers (as Mr. Carlyle used to exclaim in his less dyspeptic moments), be of good cheer. We are all together, you and I, and George III, and Henry the Eighth (a Plain Man, indeed, though troubled with insanity), and Mr. Cromwell his servant, who summarily executed the abbot of Glaston, and Mr. Bowdler, who improved the plays of Shakespeare, and the Reverend Mr. Gastrell, who hewed down Shakespeare's mulberry tree at Stratford, and my Lord North and Ivan the Terrible and Henry Ford and the Iron Duke and Attila and William Henry Poofer of Ponders End, who was the first Plain Man to enunciate the shattering ultimatum

" *I know what I like,*"

and Colonel Ramjar of the 23rd Kukris, who in

the year 1885 wrote this brief and rousing letter
to the *Timepiece* on the subject of the vergers'
strike of that year :

To the Editor of the *Timepiece*.

Sir,—I am a plain man. Let us have no
beating about the bush. Give 'em cold
steel.

Egbert Harkaway Ramjar,

Lt.-Col. (ret.).

The Primings, Cheltenham.

Are we not a gallant company ? O Plain Men,
O my darlings, let me conclude, if you please, with
a sober quotation from an eighteenth-century
moralist. " Methought " (he says) " I was carried
into a dark valley, where I perceived a young man
ascending a mountain. In his hand he bore a
banner inscribed *No D——d Nonsense* ; and to
each of his feet was chained a heavy weight, the
one inscribed *Fancy* and the other *Imagination*.
And I saw that two vultures called *Art* and *Unre-
munerative Trifling* were pecking at his vitals, and
that around him circled several figures called
Fantasy, *Poetic Folly*, etc., shooting at him with
darts. But his eyes were turned steadfastly to
the top of the mountain, where shining figures called
Practical Methods, *Solid Profit*, and *One Hundred
per Cent* leaned down to beckon him onward and
upward, amid a heavenly light. And I saw him
struggle at length to the crest and there received
with ravishing choruses sung by several *Bankers*
in vestments so dazzling that at the sight I swooned
away in rapture."

IN PRAISE OF PLAIN MEN

Little Plain Men, little Plain Men of my soul,
I leave you with a comfortable benediction out
of Dr. François Rabelais: "*Mais escoutez,
vietsdazes. . . . !*"

The Crystal Tower: A Fairy-Tale for Business Men ∽ ∽ ∽ ∽

THERE was once a stockbroker named (rather horribly) J. Gatherby Pilkington, who lost himself one stormy night in the Surrey Hills; for once you get a stockbroker off a tarred road he is doomed. The night was inky black, with a howl of rain. J. Gatherby Pilkington stumbled desperately up and down for some hours, repeating "one hundred and nine and a quarter—one hundred and eight and five-eighths," for he did not know any other prayers; and at last, drenched and buffeted and half dead with anguish, he saw a light twinkling among a clump of dark trees, and staggering towards it came eventually to the door of a low hut. He beat feebly on it. A thick earthy cough answered him. He lifted the latch, entered, and found himself staring at a Troll.

The Troll, who was elderly and extremely hairy, and had a long nose curved like a reaping-hook and red glowing eyes, stared unwinkingly at J. Gatherby Pilkington. Then, lifting with his toes a bowl of milk standing on the hob, he drank it thoughtfully. He then addressed the stock-broker as follows:

"But bookbinders' wives, I think, are less subject to vertigo."

"Can you tell me the way to Fairleigh Lodge, Hindham?" asked J. Gatherby Pilkington weakly.

" Yes," said the Troll. He blinked twice rapidly and proceeded without further delay to relate the story of

The Princess with the Glass Leg

There was once (said the Troll) a Prince whose profession it was to ride about the world rescuing Princesses in difficulty : though not indiscriminately, for having a small private income he could afford to indulge his taste. He preferred rescuing blondes.

It happened late one afternoon, as this Prince was riding through a dark forest, that he came suddenly to a castle called Dolorous Gard ; and as it was growing dark he spurred at once up to the postern and sent in his card, which was engraved thus :

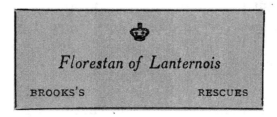

Almost immediately an aged seneschal appeared, and bowing low conducted the Prince to a chamber hung with stamped Cordova leather, in which a fire of pine-logs blazed. On a table stood two silver candlesticks, a silver flagon of Gothic shape, a manchet of bread on a silver plate, and a silver dish by Cellini containing three measly red apples. The Prince turned at once to the seneschal.

" Can I have a grilled steak ? " he asked.

The seneschal, who was as deaf as a wall,

bowed respectfully and shuffled out. Within the hour he reappeared, announcing his master, the Earl Ugren : a dry, grey, precise nobleman in the late forties.

"It is my custom, sir," began the Prince, returning the Earl's bow, "to inquire at each strange castle whose hospitality "—here he paused and glanced meaningly at the dish of apples— "whose hospitality I accept, whether I can do anything to serve my host."

The Earl Ugren reflected, and taking a note-book from his pocket fluttered the pages.

"I find," he said at length, clearing his throat, "I have a daughter named Flavia imprisoned—er —H'm. Chrm.—in a crystal tower a few leagues away. The Ogre concerned is named—er—Blup-hocks: Chrm. Chrm. Would that be out of your way ?"

"I will tell you," answered the Prince, "when I have seen her portrait." He followed his host to the picture-gallery. The Earl held a candle to the portrait of a girl with red hair. The Prince put up his eyeglass and scrutinised it carefully, in silence.

"Very well," he said at length. "I should like to be called at eight, please. China tea, with two thin slices of bread-and-butter."

His host bowed and withdrew, wishing the Prince good night. At the end of the gallery he paused, and came back again.

"There *is*, after all," he said, "just one other little thing. . . . I wonder . . . Could I . . . Could you *possibly* oblige me——"

"Good night," said the Prince, shaking him cordially by the hand.

At eight next morning the Prince rose, bathed, shaved, and was in the saddle and clattering over the drawbridge by nine. Late in the afternoon he reached a lonely inn and put up his horse. The Crystal Tower lay a mile to the east, in an impenetrable wood. At 6.35 that evening the Prince, sword in hand—

" I trust," said the Troll, " you are following the story ? " " Yes," said the stockbroker faintly. " Are you on the 'phone to Dorking ? " " No," said the Troll.

—leaped lightly through the topmost window of the tower into the Blue Room, where the Earl's daughter sat with a maid brushing her red hair.

"Please waste no time," said the Prince brusquely. The Lady Flavia rose.

"You have come (You can go, Parker) to rescue me ? " she said.

"Obviously."

"I'm so——"

"Never mind the gratitude part now," said the Prince, glancing at his watch.

"And . . . you are going to marry me afterwards ? "

The Prince examined the hilt of his sword.

"Er—that is my general rule," he answered.

The Lady Flavia bit her red lip reflectively.

"Could you possibly stay to dinner ? " she asked.

"How on earth——" The Prince stared at her.

"It's like this," said the Lady Flavia. "Stanley —that's Bluphocks, you know—wants to extend the ransom side of the business. Unfortunately some of the bereaved round here—this is a huntin' country—refuse to cough up a penny to release their beastly relatives. Consequence is the place is chock-full of bird-headed wombats and striped griffins and what not, all of them not only eating their heads off but wasting a frightful lot of good Magic every week, and the shareholders are getting sticky about it. What we really want is somebody with tact and initiative and a little capital to ride round and induce the bereaved to fork out. Some of 'em positively seem to like having aunts with feathers. . . . Ten per cent and a hundred Preference shares to start with, and, of course, what you make yourself out of the sorrowing families. What about it ? You'll stay to dinner, of course ? "

"I . . . You . . ." stammered the Prince.

" Never mind the gratitude part now," said the Lady Flavia, touching the bell.

The Troll ceased to speak, and sat crooning.

" If," said the stockbroker in a feeble voice, " there is a garage near here, I could——" ·

" She had no glass leg," said the Troll suddenly. " I only put it in for the sake of the Human Interest. As for what you say about haddocks, I prefer the Albert Hall."

With these words the Troll rose and pushed the stockbroker out into the storm again, slamming and barring the door upon him.

Spleen ↶ ↶ ↶ ↶ ↶ ↶

IN the house, overlooking the Seine, where
Voltaire died—it is now a restaurant as to the
ground floor, like Burke's house in Gerrard Street
—in this house I met a melancholy man. The
night was freezing cold. The dark and turbulent
river, fretted with golden lights, turned and ran
beneath the bridges. A pallid moon hung over
the dark mass of the Louvre. This melancholy
man sat near the restaurant stove. I knew him
to be connected with the trade (or, as some call it,
the Profession) of Letters, and took him to be
brooding over his dreadful life, and perhaps
composing; for the quarter is rich in Literature.
We have a little hotel where Baudelaire lived, and
Wagner, and Oscar Wilde; and round the corner
is Chateaubriand's house—a name revered by
every lover of steak.

I asked this man what irked him. He said
(with a groan) that he had been at a studio party
in the Quarter the night before and had lost his
guitar. He said he could not go home without
his guitar. He said he had also fallen downstairs
in the early morning. He said Love was a lie,
that the world was full of ugly faces which gave
him a pain in the neck, and that he had lost his
guitar. He had also (he added) fallen downstairs
in the early morning. With that he became as
mute as a haddock and relapsed into brooding;
and I respected his grief and left him, for I saw
that he was suffering from the malady called by
the poets (and especially the French poets, and

among them especially the Romantics and the Symbolists) *le spleen*. This is a malady of the soul, and has nothing to do with what is (I believe) an adjunct of the liver. It is a deep and appalling ennui, a weariness, a despair, an ache, a cloud. A modern English essayist has confused it with that disease of the soul which our devout fathers knew as *accedia* ; but I think he is wrong. *Accedia* was more terrible and more fleeting—a black night of the soul which came at moments to men who believed ; whereas anyone with a romantic temperament can have *le spleen*—you, and Sir Thomas Lipton, and Dean Swift, and the Mayor of Littlehampton, and the Neo-Georgians, and Grock, and little Mrs. What's-her-Name the novelist, and Lord Byron, and the old lady who sells balloons outside the Louvre. Under the influence of this malady many poems have been written, some strong, sombre, and fatal, like Baudelaire's, and others merely piffling. Among modern poets who have so written Mrs. Bundook is considered one of the finest and most sombre ; as witness her poem called " Undertones " :

> *My soul is full of slime*
> *Where all the time*
> *Strange ghoulish shapes, wavering frenziedly*
> *Rise up to take a gnaw at me ;*
> *They chew*
> *And nozzle at my torpid heart*
> *Under the lace fichu.*
> *I start*
> *And quiver at the dull sky's greying knell ;*
> *My God ! I feel like hell !*

Queen Elizabeth on her dreadful deathbed suffered from *le spleen*, and so, I think, did Hamlet Prince of Denmark, who found Life so stale, flat, and unprofitable. I do not fancy a modern alienist would certify the Prince's indisposition as madness, though no doubt the specialists at Elsinore did, and also the Special Correspondent at Elsinore of the *Pompton (N.J.) Times-Courier-Globe*, who cabled home the full story:

PRINCE HAMLET BUGHOUSE, DOCTORS DECLARE.

Heir to Throne, Given Once-Over
By Brain Champs, is
Rated Low.

"To Be or Not To Be is Question,"
Danish Hope Retorts.

ELSINORE (Den.), Friday.—" Yes, I think the boy is bughouse," said Court Physician Carl P. Guildenkranz to-day, returning from a special summons to the Castle, where every brain doctor in the country was present to give the Danish heir the once-over.

Rumour has it that the Prince has more than once declared that the King, his uncle, is a low-life, and that he will call his bluff. His Highness certainly shoots a strong line of dope concerning family matters, and at a recent theatrical performance at the Castle was seen to be snooping round not a little. No serious doubts were thrown on his mentality, however, till he was over-heard recently thinking aloud about Life, which he certainly does not consider the elephant's camisole.

Asked if the Lady Ophelia had anything to do with the case, Carl P. Guildenkranz said, " I'll say it's a wow. Oh, boy ! " -

Carl P. Guildenkranz is a nephew by marriage, once removed, of Otis H. Guildenkranz, of Pompton, N.J., and a first cousin of Mrs. Mabel Ginkel, who married Wilbur K. Ginkel, who has many relatives in New Jersey.

I doubt very much, I say, whether Hamlet was mad ; mad, I mean, in the absolute sense, conveniently, properly, and totally mad, like Triboulet the fool, to whom Panurge went for advice on his marriage. Hamlet suffered merely from *le spleen*, and nowadays would have passed unnoticed among the practitioners of the New Arts, the New Religions, the New Music, and what not. He would probably have been a novelist, and his works would have been compared with the works of the Russians, who have capitalised ennui so well, and yet so unequally. For if you read the Russians diligently—and you never know when some bleak woman or other is not going to pounce and catch you out unawares about them—you will find that they do not all despair in the same degree, nor are their souls all equally withered. This must have caused some heartburnings in the *salons* of St. Petersburg.

"I want you," an eager hostess would say, "to meet Gonoffsky. He despairs *dreadfully*."

She introduces Zogitoff to Gonoffsky, and the two literary lions glare at each other.

"You despair a great deal, I hear?" says Zogitoff at length.

"I do," says Gonoffsky coldly.

"*My* soul," says Zogitoff, coughing, "is pretty sick."

There is a silence.

"Mine is sicker than yours," says Gonoffsky sharply. "I spend half an hour each day in groaning to myself."

That is a nasty one for his rival, but he gulps and swallows a glass of vodka.

"I myself," he says at length, speaking deliberately and weighing every word, "wake at 6.30 every morning of my life and scream steadily for an hour and a half. My soul is practically dead. I don't believe in anything, and my Aunt Tania

120

hanged herself last Tuesday afternoon. We have it in the family."

At which, I imagine, Gonoffsky bursts into tears and rushes out into the Nevsky Prospekt, where we can follow him no further; for we have only just time to wind up this fascinating discussion by coming to the conclusion that *le spleen* is not a dangerous malady, and may generally be got rid of by writing bad verse; or, if you have too much public spirit for that, by one teaspoonful of Gargol, three times daily, in a glass of water. For thus does Providence save us being overrun by puling poets.

A New Arabian Episode ✿ ✿ ✿

AT Grape Street Police Court yesterday Florizel Smith, a tobacconist, of Rupert Street, W., was charged with being concerned, on the night of the 23rd inst., in the murder of an unknown man at Hampstead Garden Suburb; and also with selling cigarettes after 8 p.m. on the same date. Defendant pleaded not guilty to the second charge.

MR. BEEZLE (for the Commissioner of Police): Is Smith your right name?

DEFENDANT: Not exactly.

MR. BEEZLE: Be good enough to tell the court your right name.

DEFENDANT: My name is Florizel of Bohemia. I was until some years ago heir to the throne.

MR. BEEZLE: Is it a fact that you were forced to relinquish your claim to the throne in consequence of your being mixed up in some rather unsavoury adventures in London?

DEFENDANT (*shrugging*): As you like.

THE MAGISTRATE: I think, Mr. Beezle, I have heard of this man. Has not a writer called Stevens, or Stevenson, given some account of his conduct?

MR. BEEZLE: I fancy so, your worship. (*To defendant*): Why do you call yourself Smith?

DEFENDANT: It seemed a good sort of name for a retired Prince in the retail tobacco trade. I would have liked Gluckstein, but I found that had already been secured.

MR. BEEZLE: Very well. You were for some

time, if I recollect rightly, concerned with a dubious establishment known as the Suicide Club. Is that still in existence?

DEFENDANT: It is, in a modified form.

MR. BEEZLE: Modified?

DEFENDANT: May I remind you that as the law now stands you cannot murder a man in London after eight o'clock at night?

THE MAGISTRATE: You are confusing the issues slightly. You are charged with selling cigarettes after eight, and with complicity in murder at Hampstead Garden Suburb.

DEFENDANT (*bowing*): Thank you, sir. I knew it was something of the sort.

MR. BEEZLE: The facts are these. I will take the earlier charge first. At 6.45 on the night of the 23rd inst. a taxicab drove quickly up one of the main avenues of the Suburb and stopped outside the Lecture Hall, where all the inhabitants were listening to an address on Sex Repressions in Indoor Plants. Two men got out, placed the body of a third, face down, on the grass, got into the cab again, and were driven swiftly away. One of these men was yourself.

DEFENDANT: Quite.

THE MAGISTRATE: The body was placed face down on the grass, I take it, in order to avoid suspicion?

MR. BEEZLE: Yes, sir. I am told that a belief in grass as a health food capable of stimulating right thinking is widespread in this suburb. (*To defendant*): Can you tell the court whose body this was?

DEFENDANT: Certainly. It was this year's President of the Suicide Club, a gentleman named Toombs. The Ace of Spades had been drawn by a gentleman named Pobblethwaite. I was merely an assistant. Pobblethwaite had tried more than one way of disposing of Toombs before he thought of an ordinary crowbar and Hampstead Garden Suburb. He had taken Toombs to several cabarets and at least one notorious " Society " play, hoping to bore him to death. He had forced him at the revolver's point to read the poems of Mr. Tinkle, in the hope that he would commit sui——

THE MAGISTRATE : Mr. Beezle, Mr. Beezle, we are wasting time. Pray get on.

MR. BEEZLE : As your worship pleases. (*To defendant*) : At any rate, this unfortunate gentleman named Toombs was found dead with his mouth full of grass in Hamp——

DEFENDANT : He was a vegetarian.

MR. BEEZLE (*severely*) : *De mortuis*, Mr. Smith. And now as to this other charge. You deny serving a police-officer in disguise with cigarettes at 8.2 p.m. on the night of the 23rd ?

DEFENDANT : Absolutely.

MR. BEEZLE : Be very careful. This is a serious matter. I have forty-five witnesses. The Big Five have been engaged in this case. Be careful, Mr. Smith. Do not let your association with the late Mr. Stevens, or Stevenson, lead you to indulge in romance.

DEFENDANT (*shrugging*) : I always thought him a *poseur*. He wore a velvet jacket. As for his much-boomed literary style——

THE MAGISTRATE : Tell me, is this Suicide Club of yours a night club ?

DEFENDANT : A little jollier than most, sir, but certainly a night club.

THE MAGISTRATE : The members cut the cards to decide their fate and eventually die violent deaths at each other's hands ?

A NEW ARABIAN EPISODE

·DEFENDANT : That is so.

THE MAGISTRATE (*thoughtfully*) : A very excellent system for a London night club, too. Pray continue, Mr. Beezle.

MR. BEEZLE : I should like to say first, your worship, that in order to bring this crime home to the defendant it was necessary to rent the entire block of houses facing his shop for some weeks. Detective officers disguised as policemen, as Peers of the Realm, as old ladies, as ice-cream vendors, as district visitors, as inhabitants of Upper Norwood and South Mimms, as waiters, and what not, kept watch from the windows night and day. At the same time the street was carefully patrolled by picked men disguised as organ-grinders and Boy Scouts, and observation was also kept on the defendant's movements through holes bored in adjacent walls.

THE MAGISTRATE (*yawning*) : A very creditable performance, Mr. Beezle, and one which reflects honour on all concerned. I propose dealing summarily with this case and inflicting a fine of fifty pounds, with costs. The other case is adjourned *sine die*, and the defendant is bound over. (*To defendant*) : Will your Royal Highness do me the honour of dining with me to-night ?

DEFENDANT (*bowing*) : With the very greatest pleasure, your worship.

Shortly after which (says the aged Arab chronicler to whom I am indebted for this account) the Prince and the Magistrate left the court arm in arm, and the Magistrate was observed to accept (slightly blenching) a cigar from the Prince, remarking at the same time that it looked like thunder.

Some Definitions ∽ ∽ ∽ ∽

IT was my privilege the other day to pick up for a trifling sum a book by a Victorian Prophet : and turning at once to the back pages (as one naturally does in such cases) I found a list of publications by a still existent firm of publishers, for the year 1868.   Do you know what the wild Victorians were reading in that year ?   I will give a selection from the list.

BRIGHT.—Speeches on various Questions of Public Policy, by John Bright, M.P.

CHATTERTON.—*Leonore: a Tale*, by GEORGIANA LADY CHATTERTON ;   beautifully printed on thick toned paper, with Vignettes by JEENS.

Guide to the Unprotected, in everyday Matters related to Property, by a BANKER'S DAUGHTER. (Third Edition.)

HILL.—The Training of Juvenile Paupers.

Spring Songs, by a West Highlander.   With a Vignette.

Social Duties considered with Reference to the Organisation of Effort in Works of Benevolence and Public Utility, by a MAN OF BUSINESS.

WEBSTER (Augusta).—*A Woman Sold*, and other Poems.

Have we not here, my little friends, the Victorian Age in the hollow of our hand ?   I have passed over the chief feature of the catalogue.   When the Victorians were not guarding their property, bullying juvenile paupers, organising fearful kinds of benevolence, and dropping a tear over Georgiana

Lady Chatterton's Leonore, they were perusing (their own word. Wow!)—they were perusing sermons. Half the catalogue is sermons. Bishops (they had not then taken to journalism) flooded the market with octavo volumes at half a guinea; you could get a dean's for seven and six, and so decline in the hierarchic scale to University preachers and the rank and file, at half a crown apiece. But few of them, I observe with regret, touched the dreadful Victorians so intimately as the Banker's Daughter, jingling and rustling—I can see her enormous bangles, her cornelian ear-rings, her flounces, her eagle nose from here—masterfully into her Third Edition. What a girl! Let us hope she married the MAN OF BUSINESS and helped him to dragoon the shrinking poor; or else either

BAXTER.—National Income. With a Coloured Diagram,

or

" ECONOMICUS."—Letters on some Questions of International Exchange, reprinted from *The Times*; with considerable Additions.

I think, myself, " Economicus " was her mate. He had (I should say) a vast white forehead, gener-ally supported by a large white forefinger, and spoke in capital letters, as if issuing proclamations: " I AM UNDER THE NECESSITY OF OBSERVING, EUPHEMIA, THAT MY BARLEY-WATER WAS AGAIN BROUGHT TO ME THIS MORNING AT FOUR MINUTES PAST ELEVEN, INSTEAD OF AT ELEVEN PRECISELY, AS I ORDERED. WHY IS THIS? " Brr! He, no doubt, belonged to the Athenæum, and (as Wilde said about somebody else) had no enemies, but was extensively disliked by his friends. The right

man to cow a Banker's Daughter. Victorian
England was full of such.

Fascinating, in a fearful way, as these people
are, there is something else in this catalogue which
interested me more: a work by Dr. Chevenix
Trench, Anglican Archbishop of Dublin. It is
called *Some Deficiencies in our English Dictionary*.

I since tried to get a copy of the Archbishop's
book, but it was as difficult to find as a pair
of corduroys in the Labour Party. I wanted
it because the English language is a fascinating
and adventurous thing. If you doubt this consider a word at random—say the word " trivial."
It comes from the Latin *trivia*, meaning the places
where three ways met; the crossroads being the
favourite lounging-place for idle babblers and
gossips. " Mews," again: I should hope it is
impossible to pass a mews without seeing in a
vision the falcons moulting (*mutare, muer*) and
plunging thereby into the Age of Chivalry. I
should have liked Archbishop Trench's book
because it must have had definitions in it, and
definitions (as Dr. Johnson knew) are great sport.
The Académie Française, whose deliberations on
their great Dictionary are at this moment centred
on the *M*'s, recently had to discuss an exclamation
taxicab drivers use in anger or in some sudden
trouble of the spirit. The Academy accepted it,
and it is now part of the French language. What
fun it is! as Topcliffe the Elizabethan torturer
said to his wife.

A small English Dictionary on which I am
myself engaged at this time, between trains, will
contain the following definitions, all, I think,
fairly accurate, sound, and suited to the age:

AWFUL, a: Provocative of awe or terror.
Anything by Mr. Popstein.

SOME DEFINITIONS

ALIEN, a : Foreign, as apéritifs, logic, etc.

BARONET, n : Political economy. Something brought in by the New Year.

BULLDOG, n : A dog at once stupid and sentimental : hence, the Victorian national emblem.

CRITIC, n : One who has tried everything else.

CULTURED, a : In England, the attribute of a person who says he reads Marcel Proust. In America, of a person who says he has read *Ulysses*.

DEMOCRATIC, a : Applied to the act of blowing the nose, performed by persons above the rank of Baronet.

DEAN, n : A person diaconally performing journalistic functions.

HISTORY, n : Any book with coloured pictures.

LITERATURE, n : Prose or verse published between orange (or yellow) covers.

MEDIEVAL, a : Anything Mr. Howl doesn't understand.

NERVES, n pl : One explanation of Miss Fribble's poetry.

NERVE, n sing : Another.

PUFF, n : Hot exhalations, as of engines or Press agents.

QUAINT, a : Old-fashioned, out of date ; as hansom-cabs, courtesy, etc.

SUCCESS, n : What happens if one is not discovered first.

SCIENCE, n : Anything expressed loudly, in jargon.

VICE, n : Something that occurs abroad.

I do not pretend that these definitions are all complete. For example, *alien* is not merely foreign, but anything (e.g.) Dean Inge doesn't like, from a lizard to a crusade. A *Baronet* may not be a Baronet merely for the Party's purposes, but his own: as the saying is, Bart for Bart's sake. *Literature* may include anything written in any review sold at sixpence a copy or over: I have done it myself, and I know. Under sixpence it is journalism. The definition, however, is exact as it stands, for everything between orange (or yellow) covers is Literature; however odd that may seem. To my definition of *History* some, no doubt, would add that the pictures must be of persons *in costume*; for example, " The Conqueror Gazing on the Body of Harold " (1066). I mainly agree, for one of the purposes of History is surely to show what queer, idiotic people lived before us, and what silly clothes they wore. A *Critic*, some may say, need not necessarily have tried *everything* else. Again I agree. In my definition I assume that he has tried everything he was capable of trying: excluding, naturally, such things as making blast-furnaces, reading, and training elephants. *Medieval* has perhaps a broader meaning than I have given it; it means, generally speaking, everything people did when they were not so clever as they are now. *Quaint* may mean a little more than old-fashioned—say, something really laughable and stupid, like the tale of Don Quixote, or the Franciscan Idea: something with absolutely no punch in it whatsoever.

And so forth.

Song in Praise of St. Dunstan and Sussex

SONG IN PRAISE OF SAINT DUNSTAN AND THE
HOLY COUNTY OF SUSSEX, AND TO THE
ETERNAL CONFUSION OF THEM THAT LIVE IN
SURREY AND DO VERY DAMNABLY PEDDLE IN
STOCKS; PECCATOR VIDEBIT ET IRASCETUR;
MEET TO BE SUNG AT HOCK-TIDE AND
FESTIVALS WITH OCTAVE.

I

Saint Dunstan was a Sussex Man,
Benedicamus Domino.
He drank strong ale from a silver can,
Semper sit laudatio.
The Devil came bouncing out of Surrey
And left for home in a devilish hurry,
At Gué-de-Vède he lost his way—
He found it again at Buzançay.

Chorus

Oh, snouts are red at Wisboro' Green,
And they whack the pot like men, I ween,
In Horsham Town and Helling-ly,
In little Alfriston and in Rye.

II

The Devil he lived round Hindhead way,
Bombinans in vacuo.
He snatched five brokers' souls away,
Mortis in articulo.

131

ON STRAW

But when he got to Roundabout
They banged him silly and threw him out,
At Storrington they gnawed his ear—
They welcomed him at Haslemere.

Chorus

Oh, the lads of Sussex swagger and screech
From Ditchling Beacon to Hastings Beach,
And Sussex men do bellow and sing
From Birling Gap to Chancton Ring.

III

The Devil flew off to Périgueux,
   Tamquam leo rugiens.
By Folq-les-Rois, Fijeac, and Eu,
   Præ timore fugiens.
But Saint Dunstan he called the Sussex Men
From barn and, sheepfold, byre and pen,
From Harting, Houndsditch, Troon, and Tring,
And they roared and howled like anything.

Chorus

Oh, the brown ale foams in Uckfield inns,
And in Lewes they drink from salmon-tins,
But the Sussex lads who roar the most
Take a genteel sip and give up the ghost.

On Food   *oo*   *oo*   *oo*   *oo*   *oo*

A HUNDRED years ago there died in a house in the Rue des Filles-Saint-Thomas, in Paris, the great Brillat-Savarin (Jean-Anthelme) ; a *savant*, an epicure, a philosopher, and the author of a treatise on food and drink which is to our Mrs. Beeton's masterpiece as the Odes of Horace to an auctioneer's catalogue. I refer to "*La Physiologie du Goût.*" Let us, bringing a modest laurel to lay at the feet of Brillat-Savarin, meditate for a space on the subject of Food. There is also something to say about High Tea, but we shall come to that only too soon.

. How easy it would be to begin an act of homage to Brillat-Savarin with a huge rumble of curses against persons who browse (like rabbits) on grasses and nuts ! How easy to prove them outcast, pimply, and damned ! None of the Councils, and certainly not that of Trent, so far as I know, ever pronounced any formal ban or malediction against such persons ; but it would be terribly simple (would it not ?) to supply this need and to embrace all nut-eaters,

Ferocious nut-eaters,
Precocious nut-eaters,
Pragmatical nut-
    eaters,
Astigmatical nut-
    eaters,
Nut-eaters devoted to
  Fabian ideals,
Cryptic nut-eaters,

Nut-eaters enjoying
  rights of *sac* and *soc*,
Furtive nut-eaters,
Assertive nut-eaters,
Hyperbolic nut-eaters,
Diabolic nut-eaters,
Nut-eaters scrabbling
  in reticules for
  crumbs,

Elliptic nut-eaters,
Pedantic nut-eaters,
Sycophantic nut-
    eaters,
Hypothetical nut-
    eaters,
Arithmetical nut-
    eaters,
Meticulous nut-eaters,
Ridiculous nut-eaters,
Nut-eaters absolute
    and confirmed,

Static nut-eaters,
Lymphatic nut-eaters,
Lyrical nut-eaters,
Empirical nut-eaters,
Anticlerical nut-eaters,
Hysterical nut-eaters
Comic nut-eaters,
Atomic nut-eaters,
Nut-eaters *de bécarre
et de bémol,*
Nut-eaters seised in
    double burgage,

—to include them all, I say, in one immense, sonorous and satisfying anathema. But we are too well-disposed. The subject of Food, like that of Love, should cause the breast to heave and the cheek to flush with nothing but the gentlest emotions. And besides, we have not the time. Let us return to Brillat-Savarin (Jean-Anthelme), who was the first philosopher to make eating and drinking an exact science. Dr. Samuel Johnson (a florid eater, but a discriminating lover of Food) once intended to do this himself. " I could write," he observed while dining one day at Mr. Dilly's in the Poultry, " a better book of Cookery than has ever yet been written; it should be a book upon philosophical principles." But the Doctor never wrote this book, and the French are still under the impression that we bite and worry our meat raw.

It is to be noted that Brillat-Savarin, whose book contains so many aphorisms (for example: " The discovery of a new dish does more for the happiness of mankind than the discovery of a new star." And: " Dessert without cheese is like a beautiful woman with one eye "), has the same contempt for gulosity that the late Sir Walter Raleigh had when he wrote the beautiful lines :

> . . . *Only men in rags*
> *And gluttons old in sin*
> *Mistake themselves for carpet-bags*
> *And tumble victuals in.*

They did not believe this in the Heroic Age, and I doubt if it was pleasant to dine with the Greeks of that period. The hall would be blue with the smoke of burning grease. The floor would be red with the blood of freshly slaughtered beeves. Over the glowing hearth stood the master of the feast, hacking the meat and giving to each guest the share suited to his importance. The heroes gorged themselves stiff and drank deep from the common wine-cup ; and in her " Fireside Chat " feature in *The Achæan Mercury* Aunt Aglaia, I conjecture, gave her weekly Household Hint :

" Whatever shall I do ? " wailed a distracted little housewife to me the other day. " Kallikrates is bringing a man home to dinner unexpectedly, and there isn't a thing in the house ! "

I was able to reassure her.

" My dear," I pointed out, " any practical housewife can knock together a tasty meal at a moment's notice if she uses up the odds and ends which accumulate in every household." I thereupon gave her this recipe :

A Simple Snack

Take five bulls. Pile neatly on a brisk fire, garnish with a sprig of thyme, and serve hot.

Which brings us, however unwillingly, to the subject of High (or Meat) Tea. Alone among the white races the English practise this ; for we are a dogged and hardy people. It is true that here and there poets have been moved to melancholy by the practice, as, for example, in "A Loamshire Lad," where the sad and exquisite lines occur:

With rue my heart is laden
For many a golden lad
And many a rose-lipt maiden—
They do not know, by Gad !
That steak well steeped in tannin,
(Although it may sound rum),
Can do the strongest man in,
And oxydise his tum.

And again, from the same:

When lads were home from labour,
And Bredon Hill was brown,
A lad would tell his neighbour
And come to Ludlow town :
And though the act was septic,
And smacked of villainy,
Feeling dyspeptic
I'd give them whelks for tea.

But, as I say, we do it. High Tea has been glorified by national writers like Dickens, and the luscious meal which Mrs. Snagsby offered the Reverend Mr. Chadband is one from which imaginative men who cherish their stomachs delicately must recoil with loud cries. There was once an old lady who wrote to the great and awful "Cavendish," the whist dictator, inquiring whether teetotallers might play at Snapdragon. I should not be surprised to hear that a similar old lady had written to Brillat-Savarin saying:

DEAR SIR,—I am anxious to know if fried haddock goes with tea, or whether it is better to have lobster alone.

136

In which case the Frenchman would, I certainly think, have been justified in observing confidentially to his friends, with reference to the old lady, that she was no epicure. Yet in China, where they esteem little dogs cooked in honey and salted earthworms, I suppose they would honour her ; as also in Rome, where the *gourmets* had such a passion for dormice in syrup and singing-birds' brains.

We had meant to discuss a little (had we not ?) the art of feeding, the science of Brillat-Savarin, the delicate dishes and the fine wines of Europe. Nobody in France thinks we know anything about Food in England. It seems a bit thick, as Mr. Beeton said to Mrs. Beeton on the day she used glue in mistake for stock. However, I fancy we may at least conclude with an interesting historical hypothesis. The English buccaneers of the seventeenth century, penetrating inland to sack some town or other of New Spain, had to eat their boots, strip by strip, for lack of other food. May we assume (if it is not assuming too much) that this is the origin of High (or Meat) Tea ?

May we ? Thanks. Thanks awfully.

The Gypsy's Warning   ◎   ◎   ◎

For I gazed into the Future and as far as eye could see
Saw the something something something and the tumty yet
to be. —ALFRED, LORD TENNYSON.

Methinks I am describing :—'tis an ill habit.
                     —HORACE WALPOLE (Letters).

A TIME ago when I was wandering in Touraine—it was about the time of the British Association's meeting in England—I made a ceremonial visit to the aged Sybil of Panzoult, who gave Panurge such discomfortable prophecy concerning marriage so very long ago. I found the excellent (if snuffy) old lady still in practice as a seer, though in reduced circumstances, and very bitter against Mr. H. G. Wells and other largely advertised modern soothsayers; but at length, after the ritual foamings, starings, and wallowings, she accepted the god, and on coming out of her trance she told me the mirific things I am about to set down; namely, the wonders preparing for us all in the future by Science. O, my little ones, what wonders! Wonders of which we may well say in the words of that hymn of the Middle Ages describing Paradise (for they had then, of course, no Modern Science) :

Nec desiderio minus est præmium

—the reward does not fall short of expectation.

Let us therefore (very reverently) contemplate some of the marvels of the year 1957; for that was the year described to me by the Sybil.

1957

January

17 : Lord Bilberry, F.R.S., dies by wireless at his house in South Kensington ; aged 87.

25 : The Bishop of Hammersmith inducts a curate relatively at Putney.

February

8 : Handel's Oratorio " The Messiah " sung throughout in six minutes five and a half seconds by 170,000 voices at the Crystal Palace.

*_** This magnificent result (a speed record) is made possible by the injection into each singer of twenty grains of metagroboldehyde by Sir Plathers Plathers, K.C.B.

March

7 : Revolution in Big-Game Hunting : Lieut.-Col. Blast, reclining on a settee in the Sports Club, W., by pressing a button fires a wireless 99.9 long-distance howitzer situated in the suburbs of Durban and brings down a herd of 29 elephants at 'Nbongo, in the depths of Central Africa.

25 : Sir Porchester Chuffe, F.R.S., is enabled by means of the Mortlephore to die simultane- ously in Lancaster Gate, W., and Pogo-Pogo (Andaman Islands).

*_** The Mortlephore, the newest achievement of Modern

Science, is the invention of Lord Gripps. Until this year it was impossible to die in more than one place at once.

April, May, and June

[These three months were abolished, 1955, by a special Act of Parliament in the City interest, as taking up too much time.]

July

16 : Valuable Scientific Invention for the Rich. In the funeral chamber of Sir Z. Zimmerschein, Chairman of North British Gold Developments Ltd., the Bishop of Surbiton presses a button setting in motion the Divitimeter, in the presence of several influential members of the Stock Exchange and a fashionable and artistic gathering.

*** The Divitimeter, the invention of Professor Licking, enables Big Business Men to take their money with them when attacked by death ; an annoyance to which they were till this moment exposed. The apparatus is actuated by a positive Plützheimer Ray.

August

4 : The Upper House of Convocation, aware that it is necessary to move with the Spirit of the Times, transfers the approaching feast of Christmas to the previous June 25, thereby saving six months.

Interesting addendum to report by Archbishop of Canterbury pleading for compromise.

THE GYPSY'S WARNING

29 : Mr. Dashaway, flying a 1,000 h.p. Boomer-plane, arrives in Baghdad a week before he started from Croydon. This constitutes a speed record up to now.

OCTOBER

22 : High-Water Mark of Benefits conferred this year by Modern Science on Mankind ; namely, discovery of the Synthetic Soul by Sir Tumley Tumley, O.M.

₊ This amazing discovery, with its unspeakable possibilities, is the fruit of many weeks' experiment. By the Tumley Tumley Method the vacuum superstitiously supposed by former ages to contain the human soul (see *Int. Journ. Sc. Przg. Prog. Phys. Chem. Act.,* Leipzig, April 1889, articles Puffenbaum, Progway, Zolzt, Grablington, and Mrs. Glibberley) is filled by a synthetic " soul-solution " injected soon after birth.

The " soul-solution," which is injected with a Grüb-wasser high-tension syringe, is built up of various alkaloids and colloidal metazoitoids giving negative reactions to the Bimmerzug tests.

23 : Joy of Dean Binge. Smashing sermon against mediaeval superstitions, and deification of Tumley Tumley. International series of articles immediately booked by Dean's agent at bumper price. In an interesting interview Archbishop of Canterbury pleads for moderation, as far as consonant with modern conditions.

NOVEMBER

2 : (formerly All Souls) Sir G. Grampus, F.R.S., predicts more marvels for next year.

141

3 : World-wide crisis in the Carthusian Order owing to rush of 587,886,542 applicants for admission as postulants.

Here the Sybil ended, abruptly. It is possible that I did not catch all she said, for she mumbles in her beard a great deal, and goes off vaguely bombinating at a tangent, just like a new philosophy.

Her prophecies I regard as extremely interesting, except perhaps the last one ; for I cannot conceive (and Mrs. Bossom will concur) that people who are going to have everything so loud and so fast would deliberately plunge into medievalism to escape their happy fate. Sir O. Goldbaum, when I mentioned the merest possibility of this, was very scornful, and exclaimed several times, " *Vat do they vant then, don't it ?* " He thinks it hardly likely that the Rich, at any rate, would stoop to such folly, and I am inclined to agree. I believe we have Dean Binge with us in this, and certainly most of the City interest, and, of course, little Screwborough and the Birmingham lot. Advance bookings for the Divitimeter are already, I hear, very heavy, and Professor Licking is already designing a model which can deal not only with Gold and Notes, but also with Bonds and Securities.

Allons, then, cameradoes ! (or cameradi), as the inexpressibly tedious Whitman (Walt) bellows. The Future lies before us ! Let us, taking up something or other, manifest our what d'you call it in the great free bounding universal thingumbob. Science is at hand to guide, to urge, to reveal, to make Life faster, and higher, and thicker, and generally awful for everybody.

No, not for everybody. For when you, my

unhappy little creatures, are shooting and drowning yourselves to get away from it all I shall, I hope, be contented and at peace, and that in a manner already old when Duke William banged our fathers' faces at Hastings (1066). *Dominus vobiscum.*

Turnip-Ghosts ∽ ∽ ∽ ∽ ∽

ONE goes into a drawing-room in Chelsea or in Hampstead. One sees, prominently displayed on little lacquer tables, the plays of Pirandello and the novels of Marcel Proust. One hears the high, strained voices talking of Pirandello and Proust ; one sees the pale, glazed eyes (like those of demented hake) gloating over Proust and Pirandello. One takes leave of one's hostess and quits the house of death on tiptoe. How cowardly this is ! How wrong !

One should, of course, stand up to these things like a man. One should refuse to be intimidated. It was, I think, about two years ago that I myself, remembering that I have fought for my King, summoned up my courage and doggedly read through three volumes of Marcel Proust, beginning with *Du Côté de Chez Swann*. How shall I describe the novels of Marcel Proust ? They are like the voice of a libidinous maiden lady in a high fever talking interminably in a hothouse through three thicknesses of woollen blanket. They are as endless as the Cromwell Road. They are written in a tortured, elusive French which gives many cultivated Frenchmen a pain in the neck. M. Proust's last novel has recently been epitomised by a Parisian critic as consisting of 500 pages as tiresome as a hundred thousand—" *embêtantes comme cent mille.*" So much for one of the turnip ghosts of the intelligentsia. Henceforth I am not to be intimidated by bleak women in Chelsea and

Hampstead who whicker about Proust. I know him for what he is.

Signor Pirandello is an easier matter altogether. Once one has grasped the Pirandello method all the elaborate fencing erected round him by the highbrows falls with a dull thud to the ground. I notice that Signor Pirandello himself, lecturing at Milan the other day, attributed his play called (in English) " And That's the Truth (If You Think So) " to a nightmare which came to him in bed. It did not surprise me.

I ask you now, my little ones, for one moment, to be brave. Auntie is going to stand by you. It will not hurt. The kind gentleman will get it over quite quickly. You simply must have it done ; otherwise you will be humiliated and abashed by highbrows all your life. In a word, we are going to attack this business like men and prove, by going at it courageously, that there is nothing to be afraid of, and that the whole thing is as easy as pie. We can best do this by constructing a little play of our own from the Pirandello formula. The one we are going to make may be called

PERHAPS YOU'RE RIGHT (IF YOU SAY SO)

The bureau of the Chief Inspector of Weights and Measures in a small Italian town. The Chief Inspector, ANNIBALE POZZI, *striding to and fro in some agitation.*

There is a mirror over the weighing-machine. POZZI *stops and looks at his reflection with a sardonic smile.*

The telephone bell rings.

POZZI (*at the telephone*) : Hallo . . . Hallo . . .

Yes . . . It is Pozzi speaking. . . . I am Pozzi.
. . . At least, I am not myself, but only what
you think I am ! . . . The real me is quite
different. . . . I am just an illusion. . . . Sometimes I think I am like myself, and sometimes not.
. . . What ? Not at all. . . . Thank *you*. . . .
Good-bye.

[*Hangs up the receiver. A* STOUT WOMAN *enters
and weighs herself on the weighing-machine.*]

THE STOUT WOMAN (*stridently*) : Sixteen stone.

[*Goes out smirking.*]

POZZI (*pondering*) : Illusion ? Is she real ?
What is her dimension ? It depends !

[*The* PREFECT *enters, withdrawing his gloves.*]

THE PREFECT : Good morning. I hear you
have done away with your wife.
POZZI (*shrugging*) : She only thinks she is done
away with.
THE PREFECT : Come ! She was alive last week.
POZZI (*kindly*) : She thought she was. She
seemed so to me, to you, to everybody. But—
was she ? Or did she, we, you, I, all of us just
think she was real ? The illusion of reality; or
the reality of illusion ?
THE PREFECT (*a trifle staggered*) : Ah ! Thank
you.

[*Goes out thoughtfully. The* STOUT WOMAN
*re-enters and weighs herself again. As she
steps off the weighing-machine and lifts her
veil* POZZI *sees that she is his mother-in-
law.*]

THE STOUT WOMAN : Ah ! Ah ! So it is you !
POZZI (*toying with her*) : Practically.

146

TURNIP-GHOSTS

THE STOUT WOMAN : You know me ?

POZZI : How can I say that ? You are probably invented by somebody !

[*The* STOUT WOMAN *beats on her bosom.* POZZI *shakes hands with himself thoughtfully.*]

You understand ? We all live in our own world. What I say to you has a value according to my world ; you give it a sense according to yours. One thinks one is, but one isn't ! It all depends.

THE STOUT WOMAN (*impressed*) : That sounds rather clever.

POZZI (*modestly*) : Doesn't it ?

[*At any other time the* STOUT WOMAN *would add,* " *Anyhow, George, I think you are going barmy.*" *But it flashes across her mind that this may be a Pirandello situation, and she looks at* POZZI *with respect.*]

THE STOUT WOMAN : At any rate you are Annibale Pozzi.

POZZI (*raucously*) : To-day, yes ! But to-day's realities are to-morrow's illusions !

[*The* STOUT WOMAN, *who had intended to accuse him of doing away with her daughter, gives it up. At that moment the principal* CITIZENS *of the little town, headed by the* PREFECT, *file into the bureau.*]

THE PREFECT : Good morning. We hear you have done away with your wife.

POZZI : In a relative way, perhaps.

THE STOUT WOMAN (*gloomily*) : He catches everybody out like that.

[*Relieves her feelings by weighing herself again.*]

POZZI : In front of a mirror, who can say which

is himself? We think we are one, but we are a hundred, a thousand!

[*General stupor. On the fringe of the crowd several* CITIZENS *begin to snore gently. The* PREFECT *pulls himself together.*]

THE PREFECT: Come! What we thought was your wife, is she or is she not done away with? Did she seem to you to be done away with? I mean, was she, comparatively speaking, real when she existed in your idea. . . . I mean to say, were you an illusion—No. Wait a minute.

[*Wipes his forehead.*]

That is to say, did one of you . . . Did what she appeared to you to be . . . Did . . . Oh, *blow*!

POZZI: Perhaps you're right!

[*The* CITIZENS *file slowly out again, except the* STOUT WOMAN, *whose mind has become a little unhinged, and who executes a fox-trot round the weighing-machine.*]

POZZI (*sombrely, addressing the air*): If you say so!

CURTAIN

It will be readily observed children, that this is what is called Cerebral Drama, rather than the drama of intrigue and action. If it may be thought that we have overdone the mystification *motif*, let us quote the actual concluding lines of " And That's the Truth (If You Think So) " :

MME. PONZA (*slowly and pitilessly*): What? The truth? The only truth is this—I am the daughter of Madame Frola.

OMNES (*with a sigh of satisfaction*): Ah !

MME. PONZA (*continuing*) : And the second wife of M. Ponza.

OMNES (*astonished and disappointed, in low voices*) : Oh ! How is that ?

MME. PONZA : Yes. And to myself . . . nobody. Nobody !

THE PREFECT : Ah ! No ! To yourself, madame, you must be one or the other !

MME. PONZA : No ! To myself I am . . . the person people think I am.

[*She throws through her veil a proud glance at the company and goes out. A silence.*]

LAUDISI : There you are, ladies and gentlemen ! There are the accents of truth——(*He darts a glance of ironic defiance.*) Are you satisfied ? (*He bursts out laughing.*) Ah ! ah ! ah ! ah !

CURTAIN

The thing is to end on that " Aha ! " sort of note. Outside, no doubt, Pirandello's characters take each other aside and say, " Seriously, though. What's it all *about* ? " They do not know. We do not know. You, she, and it do not know. As it says in the rhyme about the goose-girl reading Schopenhauer to her flock :

Neither do they. Neither does she.
Nor (for the matter of that) does he.

Well, well. It did not hurt much, did it ? And that is the other turnip-ghost, my dears.

The Lapse ∽ ∽ ∽ ∽ ∽

AT Grape Street Police Court yesterday an elderly female, Britannia Warboy (61), was charged with creating a disturbance outside the Army and Navy Stores, Victoria Street, S.W. Defendant, who was respectably dressed in shabby black and carried a beaded reticule, pleaded guilty.

Police-Sergeant Struggles said that he saw the defendant playing a banjo and singing on the kerb outside the Stores. When requested to move on she called him a fat, flat-footed gravel-whacker. He then took her into custody.

THE MAGISTRATE : Five shill——

MR. BROODY (*for the defence*) : Your worship will perhaps allow me to make a statement. This is a very painful case. The defendant, hitherto a woman of respectable character, for many years acted as Muse to a very well known Poet. She is an accomplished performer on the banjo and has an extensive repertoire of patriotic songs, and also hymns. Her employer gives her the best of characters.

THE MAGISTRATE : What was she singing outside the Army and Navy Stores ?

MR. BROODY : A hymn, sir. The chorus is " Lest We Forget." It is her favourite, next to " Sock 'im on the ear, Sargint, sock 'im on the snout." Both are her own composition, and she is naturally proud of them.

THE MAGISTRATE : Five shilli——

MR. BROODY : With your worship's permission I should like to call one or two ladies present to give evidence as to the defendant's character. They are all in the same line of business.

Miss Prudence Boddice, who described herself as a Seventh Day Jebusite, said that she was Muse to Mr. J-HN DR-NKW-T-R. She knew the person charged by sight, though they did not attend the same conventicle. As an expert in hymnology she recognised the tune the defendant was singing, but she thought it should have been accompanied on an Harmonium. The Banjo, even in the hands of abstainers from liquor, was not a fitting instrument.

Miss Perpetua Dudgeon, Muse to Mr. TH-M-S H-RDY, said that she had been the prey of invisible Forces since birth. · They had blasted her life, and she thought nothing mattered. She did not believe in——

THE MAGISTRATE (*yawning*) : I see. Five sh——

MR. BROODY : Begging your worship's pardon, I have two more witnesses.

Miss Daffodil Blastworthy, Muse to Mr. J-HN M-S-F-LD, said she did not hear the defendant using bad language. She (witness) would have known it directly had there been any. She (witness) knew all there was. She believed the defendant was fond of the company of soldiers. She (witness) preferred sailors. There was no accounting for tastes.

Mrs. Martha Whicker, Muse for many years to Mr. ALFR-D N-Y-S, said that speaking as one to whom Imperial Poetry was a precious, nay, a sacred charge, she——

THE MAGISTRATE : Fi—— Any more, Mr. Broody ?

MR. BROODY : I should like your worship's permission to call the defendant herself.

Mrs. Britannia Warboy, the defendant, called, expressed her sorrow at the occurrence. She had acted as Muse to her employer for more than forty years, giving entire satisfaction. A recent paragraph in the evening newspapers about a threatened outbreak of peace in Central Europe had sent her (in her own words) "all of a doo-dah," and meeting a soldier friend in the street she accompanied him to Hampstead Heath, where she relieved her indignation by dancing for some time. They also exchanged hats. She had only taken a little drop of gin, and did not recollect how she got to Victoria Street with her banjo. The hymn she was singing outside the Army and Navy Stores was composed by her employer at her suggestion. She was fond of singing to the banjo, but her voice had become a little cracked lately.

The Magistrate imposed a fine of Five Shillings, or Seven Days. The fine was paid by a gentleman in court named O. Rubenstein, who described himself as a sympathiser.

A Most Excellent Ballad of the Dairy-Mayd of the South

or,

A Rare Example of a Mayd dwelling at
Slugwash in Sussex, who for Despite of a
Gentleman of Rutlandshire went beyond Sea in the Habit of a Mar-
riner and becom a Pyrat, and
after marry'd a Baronett
of London, and now
dwelling at
Slugwash in
Sussex aforesaid.

To the tune of " Hey, upsee Joan."

(From the black-letter in the Library of the Ratoners'
Company of the City of London, *cum privilegio Regis*.)

I

Slugwash lieth
in Sussex.

There was a lovely Mayd
In Slugwash shee did dwell,
Who lov'd a Gentle-man
Of *Rutland*, as they tell..

But when he sail'd away
And left her all forlorn,
With rage her Bosome heav'd,
Her eyes flash'd all in scorn.

153

ON STRAW

The Mayd is
welcom'd
by sevrall
Marriners.

Shee came to *Portsmouth*-Hard,
Where marineers shee spied,
To whom shee told her Tale;
The honest Tarrs reply'd:

" Come hither, Doxie fair,
And sail along of wee,
Then of this bitter Wrong
Thou shalt avengèd bee."

Their Captayn
becomes
freshe;

Up spoke their Captayn then,
And with a sawcie Leer,
Ay, ay (quoth hee) my Duck,
My lollie Jade, my Dear.

Whereat the Mayd, who much
Of her good Name did reck,
Catch'd up a marlin-Spike,
And laid him on the Deck.

and is justly
Punish'd.

Quoth shee, ' Ile have you know
Ile not stande for such Gear ';
And as the Captayn dyed
The seamen gave a Cheer.

Therewith in one accord
They begg'd the Mayd to bee
Their Captayn to command
And sail upon the sea.

Saylors doe
not
care.

Ay, ay (cry'd she), my boyes,
I am a Sussex Girle;
Lay aft, you tarry Puts,
Haul bowlines and unfurle.

154

And soe they sail'd away,
While all did curse and sweare ;
The Mayd did them forbid,
But saylors doe not care.

II

They are
attack'd by
a Pyrat.

It fell upon a day
They sail'd by *Barbary*.
And lo ! a Pyrat there
Hove at them on the lee.

The fighte was long and sore,
The blood ran down in showres,
The Mayd with careful Zeale
Cut throates for sevrall houres.

Hee offers
the Mayd
marriage.

The Pyrat then cry'd ' Ho,
Since wee have won this Fighte,
Wilt marry mee, fair Mayd ? '
The Mayd reply'd ' All righte.'

' But beare in Minde (quoth shee)
I am no fancy Miss,
Tho' I have foughte all day
I am not used to this.'

Hee is
a
Bigamist.

At this the Pyrat swore
Shee'd bee his only Bride
(For what is one Wife more
When hee has twelve beside ?)

Shee marry'd him next day,
A Mullah them did wed,
With most outlandish Grinnes.
And waglings of the Head.

ON STRAW

The Mayd is
opprest with
theologick
Doubts; soone
resolv'd.
But when the Knot was tyed
She felt some lingring Doubt
As whether it were righte,
And what it was aboute.

But Lord! (quoth shee) the Girle
That weds a Pyrat must
Not quiz a Giften Horse,
But take something on Trust.

III

Shee discovers
her former
Love;
Now in a frightful Cage,
Deep in the Pyrat's Barke,
There lay a Gentle-man,
Chain'd in the horrid darke.

The Mayd in tripping past
The Prisoner did spie,
At which he turn'd his Head
And cry'd out loud, ' 'Tis I.'

and gives
him
the Birde.
' 'Tis I, my honey Sweete,
Thy Love that sail'd from thee,
Thy Gentle-man, dear Chucke ';
The Mayden said, ' I see.'

Then hastning up the staire
Shee hail'd the Pyrat, who
Heard all her eager Tale,
And told her what to doe.

Hee is solde
for
5s.
Next day with horrid Oathes
The Gentle-man so bold
Was haled up from Belowe,
And for a Slave was sold.

' Alack (cry'd hee), deare *Sue*,
What means this angry Frowne ?
What hast thou sold mee for ? '
Shee answer'd him ' A Crowne.'

' I hope (quoth shee) theyle drive
And trusse you like a Hogg ;
You'll ne'er see *Rutland* more—
Cheer-Hoe, you dirty Dogg.'

She shoulde
have helde for a
rising Markett.

Shee gazed upon her Love
And choaked within her Throate
To think shee might have asked
At least another Groate.

The Gentle-man is gone,
Shee doth herselfe bedeck
With Gew-Gaws from the Holde,
Pacing upon the Decke.

The Authour
reprobates
her frenzie.

O stonie-hearted Wench !
O mercenarie Jade !
To treat a Lover soe,
And underselle the Trade !

Is this a Sussex tricke ?
Nay, Sussex-Girles are kinde
(So Sussex poets do bawle
With an united Minde.)

Shee was
probablie a
Brighton
Girle.

Yet stricken meerly Dumb
They stubbornly ignore
The Truth that *Brighton*-towne,
Doth stand on Sussex shore !

157

ON STRAW

If shee's a *Brighton*-Girle
Shee'll not make much ado
(Her Lover beeing solde)
To selle the Pyrat too.

[*Cætera desunt.*]

On Dislike, and So Forth

THE actual title should have been " Some Reflections, Casual and Congratulatory, on Discovering Oneself to be Disliked by a Painter named Percy." But this title is perhaps a little florid, a trifle rococo ; and I am informed, moreover, that the special hand-cut type, surrounded by Cupids, scrolls, and arabesques, in which I wanted the " *Percy* " printed is obtainable only at great expense. Hence the shortened form, like prayers at sea. And hence (regretfully) we are compelled to devote ourselves to a merely general survey of this fascinating subject.

There can be no doubt that dislike is an excellent thing, and if expressed well, and without that excess which is the negation of all Art, can be of itself admirable, like the Fifth Symphony, and the Book of Kells. In an English village where I once lived for a time there was a man, a dark, secret, black-avised sort of man, living by himself at the far end by the mill, who was suspected on good grounds of having done away with two of his wives. This made him disliked by the villagers ; but their intemperate and violent manner of expressing their dislike was shocking to a polite ear, and artistically (I thought) a crime. The same applies (e.g.) to the screaming abuse exchanged between Luther and one or other of his friends and colleagues : for Luther, when he was not truckling to the rich, could be excessively abusive in a Low German way. How much more exquisite are the dislikes of Whistler, so enchantingly set forth in that manual of conduct " The Gentle Art of Making Enemies " !

It can never be too firmly impressed on those about to dislike that mere rudeness is not only a waste, like all violence, but actually distressing to the object of their dislike. It also tends to affect adversely the style, to confuse, to render muddy the clear stream of thought. Avoid it, my dears. Remember the Nun's Lament for Philip Sparrow, whom the cat killed.

> Heu, heu, me,
> *That I am woe for thee !*
> Levavi oculos meos in montis ;
> *Would that I had Xenophontis*
> *Or Socrates the wise*
> *To show me their devise*
> *Moderately to take*
> *This sorrow that I make.*

Moderation, balance, and a detestation of excess —these are cardinal principles and Matter of Breviary for those who would dislike.

I recently picked up an old Norman song-book containing an excellent example of the sort of dislike the neophyte should most passionately avoid. In the year 1514, as you must know, Louis XII sent into Normandy a body of some 6,000 German mercenaries to oppose a threatened invasion by the English. These mercenaries were called the Lansquenets, and large numbers of them were quartered on the noble town of Caen. They were generally howling drunk. Here, in my rough English, are the first two verses of a Chant Royal made on the subject by a certain Master Pierre de la Longne of Caen in that year :

> *Abominable persons ! guzzling hogs,*
> *Living a life of guile and gluttony !*

ON DISLIKE, AND SO FORTH

You think in your dull brains, you oafish dogs,
You can oppress our worthy town and free
That has so long enjoyed her liberty ?
Now do you mean to trouble us ?   What ?   Hey ?
Be off, you filthy hounds of Lansquenets.

If they could bear your presence at Bayeux,
At Argentan, and Sès, and at Falaise,
It does not follow (Saints ! what fools they were !)
That we shall stand your foul rampaging ways.
(This fact may baffle you—perhaps amaze)
We are not mangy beggars in the hay—
Be off, you filthy hounds of Lansquenets.

Observe the frenzy, the over-emphasis, the heat.
Fie ! fie ! Now listen to the more endurable
Envoy—for I omit two very horrible fierce verses.

Envoy

Prince, twenty pots of ale they each can drink,
Not counting wine, the which they swig all day ;
Cider and beer alike goes down the sink.
Such as would put much better men away. . . .
Be off, you filthy hounds of Lansquenets !

I have taken the trouble to put this into English
verse for a warning, in the sacred cause of Art.
There was once a master of Style, whose name. I
forget at this moment (Flaubert ? Maupassant ?),
whose formula was " Take hold of Eloquence and
wring its neck." Let every ardent young man on
the threshold of a Career, casting about for some
one to dislike, cut this sentence neatly out with
scissors (or even a pocket-knife ; but see that the
blade is thin, or the paper will ruck, and you will
have messed up the whole thing) and paste it
above his desk   Sobriety, Form, Restraint—these
are the watchwords.

ON STRAW

We may now consider a much more admirable specimen of dislike. I take it from a poem by Samuel Butler, who went into the Museum at Montreal and found a cast of the Discobolos hidden away in a dirty attic where an old man was stuffing an owl. Butler composed a long lament over this, for the old man explained to him that the Discobolos was rather improper. I quote only verse V :

The Discobolos is put here because he is vulgar—
He has neither vest nor pants with which to cover his limbs ;
I, sir, am a person of most respectable connections,
My brother in law is haberdasher to Mr. Spurgeon.
                    O God ! O Montreal !

Save for that last subdued wail, or moan, there is, as you see, no hint of agony or stress in this verse of dislike. It bears the stamp (in fact) of the artist.

And now lastly—though we have not touched even the outer lining of the fringe of this immense subject ; but Life is short—there is the element of Chance, or Luck. It is not in the capacity of a man to say, with sparkling eyes, " I should like to be disliked by this person, and this, and this." Alas ! The Fates will not always answer such a prayer. It happens, often, that a man is actually liked by the most terrible persons. (" I can conceive no more humiliating situation," said Beauclerk to Boswell, " than to be clapped on the back by Tom Davies.") On the contrary, it may happen that a man is both fortunate and happy, and disliked by the right people. Then what could one wish more than to have engraved on one's tomb such an epitaph as this ? —

162

ON DISLIKE, AND SO FORTH

He Lived a Long and Agreeable Life,
and was Disliked Intensely
by
Several Business Magnates, a Vorticist, a
Couple of Dramatic Critics, several
Levantines, five Best Selling Novelists,
a retired General, two Psycho-Ana-
lysts, two Vegetarians, a Female
Poet, three Publicity Agents,
two Neo-Georgians, one
Inhabitant of Chelsea,
ten Sycophants,
and thirteen
Prigs.

Fortunate senex !

So. On the day when I close my eyes on this
odd world, with (I hope) a not too wry smile, and
possibly one final serene observation, carefully
hoarded for that moment ; when at last the black
velvet cloth, spangled with silver tears, is removed,
and the tapers extinguished, and the sprinkling
done, and all said ; then let some friend stand forth
under the cypresses and say or sing in a clear voice,
with no twiddles or fal-lals, but strongly, and to
the First Plainsong Tone, not drawlingly, *tractim*,
but briskly, *raptim*, the words I have written
above.

But if I die rich (which is unlikely, by Gosh !)
I will have them set to a gay, sardonic tune I know
out of the Manuscript of Bayeux, and it shall be
loudly sung in procession at my funeral by twenty
singing-men and as many boys, with all the little
dogs of London dancing and barking in chorus.

For it is good to have innocent pleasure right
up to the end.

The Eleventh Hour ﾟ ﾟ ﾟ

Strange fits of Passion I have known.
　　　　　　　　　—WM. WORDSWORTH.

"AND, of course," murmured the doctor, pausing to scratch his nose with his fountain-pen, " no wine."

He continued writing. I gazed at my poor friend.

" No wine," said my poor friend.

" None," said the doctor.

He finished his prescription with a flourish, rose, observed that it looked confoundedly like rain, shook hands, and went briskly away.

It is necessary to be precise in this matter. The exact amount of wine bibbed by my poor friend, day in and day out, for the past twenty years has been less than half a bottle at luncheon and as much at dinner : in all, say, about five, or (at the most) six glasses of wine a day. He has fixed this frugal amount to suit his temperament and his palate, which is the kind of palate Heaven occasionally bestows on the deserving, enabling them to taste in one slow reflective sip of a fine Richebourg, or a Corton, or a Chambertin, or a Nuits, or a Vouvray, not only the grape and its bloom but also the gold in the sun which warmed it, the turquoise in the sky of Burgundy, or Hérault, or Touraine under which it ripened, the breeze, the laughter of the sunburnt vintagers, the richness of the good earth, the——

But what am I saying? The man has such an exquisite palate that there is given him, in sipping, a vision, the vision of the March through Asia, when Bacchus went before, in his car drawn by six panthers, Bacchus, young and flushed as a cherry, Bacchus in his gilt buskins and his crimson mitre garlanded with vine-leaves, laughing and terrible, and behind him the rout of Bacchantes and Fauns, Satyrs and Sylvans, Ægipans and Agripans, leaping and clashing their cymbals and dancing: and old Silenus also, pot-bellied and blinking in his woman's gown, and belabouring his ass: and he who bore the Serpe, the Holy Vineyard Knife, smithied in Heaven (as it says in the Vineyard Song) by Vulcan,

De fin acier, trempé en bon vin vieulx.

—of fine steel, tempered in old good wine. All these things this man, my poor friend, could see as he took his glass, and, first inhaling its aroma and praising God, allowed a little wine to roll round his tongue. Sometimes (if it were allowed him) he would see the walls around him melt into a summer sea, and upon it a little dancing ship, around whose mast a living vine suddenly twined, while the rigging and stays blossomed suddenly into swags and festoons of grapes both gold and purple gleaming like jewels; until, with the pouring of a great flood of purple wine across the deck and a new fragrance in the air, he would hear a great cry and see the affrighted crew leaping into the sea, and Dionysos himself standing on the poop. All these things he saw, and exulted greatly over the Business Men with glazed eyes gulping their port in the Trocadilly.

Judge therefore what "No wine" meant to such a man.

He retired into the country, to a cottage lent him for the purpose, for a month, the duration of his servitude ; at the same time cursing his Liver, and also the Great War. I knew him to be suffering. He is not the sort of man to inflict upon his civilised palate the fire-water of the Scots, still less the dreadful petrol-and-hair-oil philtres of the Americans. Beer he esteems good enough for beer-drinkers, and no more. He therefore would taste nothing but clear spring water, and also weak China tea : for coffee was forbidden him. At the end of this month he sent me a telegram asking me to spend the last week-end with him. He met me on the cottage step, looking (I thought) healthy, but having in his eyes an odd expression. On seeing me he burst into a high-pitched giggle and exclaimed :

"Oh, do you know, the League of Nations——"

So saying he led me indoors. He fussed about with a pile of books for a time and suddenly turned and said, giggling as before :

"Oh, I say, how lovely 'Abraham Linc——' "

I took the book from him and thrust him into a chair. He began at once talking feverishly about the Betterment Bookshop by the theatre in Hampstead, tonsil-drill and Greek plays for villagers, the Guild of Free Young Hearts, and community deep-breathing. He said Eurythmics were splendid, and Mrs. Grabshaw's national scheme superb, superb. Then he snatched up a little yellow review and cried, giggling loudly :

"Oh, dear, such delightful thinking by Midd——"

At that I got to grips with him. After a

brisk ten minutes he rose, dusted himself, rubbed his eyes, yawned, and said:

"Where am I? Oh, yes, I remember. What have I been saying?"

I told the poor oaf. He relapsed into deep meditation, and then addresssed me as follows:

"Perhaps you're right. I have had some rather queer experiences. I came here, you know, a little unstrung—nerves and all that. The day after I arrived I was sitting in this room alone at tea-time. I had been walking hard all day, and was thirsty, and I had drunk about five cups of weak tea. Suddenly I found my hand stretching out *of its own volition* to this bookshelf and taking down 'Oliver Cromwell.' I read at first mechanically, but later found myself joining lustily in one of the hymns in that play. I thought this odd, but realised that I was run down and needed rest and sleep. Next morning after breakfast I went at once—I was not master of my actions, but moved by some Power outside me—to the writing desk there and wrote to the secretary of the Upward Society's Bookshop, ordering these books."

He took a list from his pocket. I read:

1. *Songs of Soothing from Rabindranath Tagore (pale-blue Yapp, with fancy book-marker).*
2. *The Ethical Diary for 1927 (Art-green, limp).*
3. *Daily Aspirations, from the Mabghnàgatabha of Vind. (Purple lambskin, with pencil.)*
4. *"Under the Bonze"; a book of Thoughts from the East, by O. G. Catchpole.*

"My Faith!" I said, appalled.

He chattered on, feverishly.

"Since then I've been able to read nothing but that sort of thing. All my thoughts are ethical and pale-blue, with fancy book-markers. I am full of Hygiene and High Thinking and Rhythmics, blast them! The worst came yesterday, when I picked up this " —he pointed to the little yellow review—" and found myself reading it aloud, masticating each syllable and breathing deep between every sentence. Heaven help me."

He groaned and buried his face.

I said : " Come, come. It is not as bad as all that. You have been the victim of certain influences. Somebody from Bloomsbury has lived here before you. And of course all that weak tea——"

" Simple Greek reactions," he said in a hollow voice, " may be instilled into the villagers by teaching them to *dance* all their aspirations."

He rose and performed a series of ghastly Bloomsbury-Greek evolutions around the room, nodding and smiling, a fixed, toothy, and horrible smile.

" We have," I said, looking at my watch, " thirty minutes to catch the six-fifty-five to Town. You will pack a bag now."

By nine-fifteen the man was healed, and the wild Bloomsbury look had vanished from his tortured eyes. He also recited in a low, joyous voice *Huc, pater O Lenæe*. It was done with a little Romanée-Saint-Vivant of the right year : a little tiny wine for very good men.

On Content ∽ ∽ ∽ ∽ ∽

*Better a handful of dry dates and content therewith than to own the Gate of Peacocks and be kicked in the eye by a broody camel.—*Arabian Proverb.

THERE was once (this story is old) a very rich old Man who had a poor young Nephew. One day the poor young Nephew said suddenly to his rich old Uncle, " Pray, Uncle, why is it that although you are so rich you nevertheless invariably travel Third Class on the railways of our beloved land ? " Whereupon the rich old Man, turning viciously upon his poor young Nephew, replied in a voice like the screech of a rusty iron gate : " Because there's no Fourth, you Fool."

There was once (I am beginning a new story) a very rich and powerful Man sitting in his private office in the City, surrounded by large numbers of serfs to whom his nod was the Law : for he was not only powerful but also infallible—and not, mark you, with the strictly-defined and carefully-limited infallibility of the Pope, but an infallibility illimitable, perpetual, unshakeable, and unquestioned ; like Mr. H. G. Wells's. There entered one day a tall stranger into the palatial Outer Offices of this powerful Man, requesting an immediate interview. A private secretary came out at length.

" Have you an appointment ? " asked the secretary.

The tall stranger made no reply, but stood immovable.

" Then I'm afraid," said the secretary, turning away, " Sir William will not see you."

The stranger drew himself up to an immense height, so that he seemed to fill the world ; and removing from his face the cloak which had muffled him, revealed a stark head terrible with majesty, and unearthly power, and doom, and high dread.

" My name," he said, in a trumpet voice, " is Death."

" Fill up this slip, please," said the secretary.

The end of it was that Death had to retire discomfited to his House of Shadows : for you cannot rush in and demand to see the rich and powerful as easily as all that. Sir William was very angry about the whole affair.

Consider that the two founders of the Mendicant Orders had no need to embrace Poverty, but did so with joy ; both of them being men of family—Francis a Bernadone, but Dominic of the military family of the Guzmans, of high Visigothic descent and of the old Spanish Blood-Royal. Do not make the horrid mistake of imagining Spaniards or such race to be swarthy ! They are fair, with blue eyes and white skins. These two men had two precious things (among others) in their possession as they trudged along in that Southern heat in their scrubby habits of coarse stuff, girdled with rope : one was Courtesy. and the other Content. And this brings me (at last) to my subject—namely, the exquisite pleasure enjoyed by poor men in that Content of theirs, which is the rich fruit of Going Without.

I wish I could describe to you, my dear little people, the thrill of almost sensual delight which stabs me as I indulge myself in Going Without (for example) Miss Fribble's poems, the last important offering of Mr. Ponderby, the vital psychological studies (" Grip, amaze, leave the reader breathless "

ON CONTENT

—Mr. Yelp, in *The Sunday Sycophant*) of Mrs. Rubbage. I hear from far off the screams and gurgles of ecstasy . . . and deep within me there speaks a very tiny, very cosy voice, murmuring: "I say, you know—*you haven't got to read any of this.*" And at that my immortal soul cries "Whoops!" like an hysterical lady accompanied by a sailor; and all my heart with pleasure fills, and dances with the daffodils. The pleasure is so extreme, the Content so voluptuous, that I might almost fear it were harmful, were it not that what the medievals called the Seven Deadly Sins were abolished a few years ago by a Viennese Jew. Observe that the Content of poor men has caused to be written some of the prettiest poetry in the world.

> *Low is my porch, as is my fate ;*
> *Both void of state.*

That was written in Devonshire, in the time of Charles the Second. There is a much older poet who gave himself praise on account of his being able (and so am I) to go without such things as ceilings panelled with gold and ivory—

> *Non ebur neque aureum*
> *Mea renidet in domo lacunar*

—and great beams from Hymettus, and what not. But observe that this poet was able to do himself well (such was his Content) in other ways, for he had a little silver in his house, and a sweet-smoking altar in his garden, and a laughing girl named Phyllis, and a jar of Alban wine—not so suave or perfumed a wine, perhaps, as the rose-red Rhætian of the western Alps, but anyhow good enough to offer any girl named Phyllis. I could here, if I liked, bring up a whole troop of poets in support, but Sir G. Bools tells me the Public will not stand it—by which he means a long line of fat red men engaged in doing each other down. Therefore I will simply display in an egotistical manner a few of the things which give me my own Content, but are denied to the rich, very properly. For example :

A Head full of Fancies, mostly useless ;
Two Legs for walking the world ;
The power of making up ánd singing Rude Songs about Levantine Financiers.
A great many Memories ;
Large masses of Poetry, both new and old ;
An Instrument for removing stones from Horses' Hooves : if so be that I possessed a horse ;
A Faith ; and a Hat stained with travel ;
The *Bucolics*, bound in parchment :
A French Knife for stabbing at my enemies and carving inscriptions on trees ;
Friends ;
Several Lampoons, very tart, against leading Charlatans ;
A Spanish Gourd of goat-skin : but I have lost this ;
One Resolution never yet broken, though sorely tried a few weeks ago at the Savoy ;
A number of Imprecations, curiously fashioned, gathered in places inaccessible to the rich ;
A book of Songs ;
A quantity of black Maryland Tobacco, very rank ;
The *Dies Iræ*, with the Plain-Song proper to it ;
One or two strong Hates, as sweet as great Loves, but enduring ;
A passion for Sausage-and-Mash ;
Boswell's *Life of Johnson* ;
An engraving from the *Dance of Death*, after Holbein, showing antic Death grinning behind the Emperor on his throne : very suitable to remind a man of his end ;
The pleasures of tasting Food and Wine, of Verse (but, of course, not Mr. * * * *'s), of Rain, Roads, Fools, and a thousand other things.

And yet, you know, there are joltheads going

up and down envying a multi-millionaire like Sir B. Zaharoff and desiring his wealth! Which is ridiculous and contemptible, for with the merest fraction of it I could buy more pleasure than if I were rich : an eighth, say.

Bless you.

Divertissement : A Christmas Morality ♀

THE scene is the Renaissance ballroom of the Plaza Hotel. The time, a quarter to twelve on Christmas Eve.

The Gala Supper, tŏ be followed by the Gala Dance and Cabaret, is just finishing. All round the immense shining space of the dance floor stand small tables, lit by clusters of pink-shaded electric candles. At one end is a gallery where a band is playing soft music. At the other end is a low platform on which the Alabama Six, each of whom is paid £100 a week for producing noises from a saxophone, are presently due to perform. From a hidden lighting-chamber above an elaborate mechanism floods the entire ballroom, or any given part of it, with rich combinations of crimson, lilac, orange, gold, emerald, and rainbow lights.

Noiseless waiters glide in and out of the little tables carrying trays of liqueurs. Behind them tread other noiseless waiters carrying trays heaped with false noses, rattles, squeakers, toy drums, streamers of coloured paper, and hats of coloured paper in various shapes ; also balloons, some gilt and some brightly coloured. The intention of these is to cause the citizenry to lash themselves into a frenzy of fun, and the mind which has ordered them to be distributed is rewarded with £3,500 a year for thinking it out. All over Europe the same psychological move is being simultaneously carried out at this hour ; which shows that Genius knows no frontiers.

But this, however attractive, is not all. Punc-

DIVERTISSEMENT

tually, on the stroke of twelve an entirely new and brilliant *divertissement* is promised. The exact nature of this has been jealously guarded.

The guests at the Plaza to-night are not, it seems, a mass of nerves due to the suspense and excitement of waiting for the *divertissement* to begin. Some of them are yawning already. Others are listlessly sipping coffee and gazing at the floor.

A BORED WOMAN : What's next ?
A YOUNG MAN : I don't know. It's a secret. Something out of the ordinary.
THE BORED WOMAN (*yawning*) : What rot. They're all the same.
THE YOUNG MAN : You wanted to come here.
THE BORED WOMAN : One must go somewhere.

[*They are silent.*]

A VERY YOUNG MAN (*consulting programme*) : Who's Dinkie Dawn ?
ANOTHER V. Y. M. : Never heard of her.
FIRST V. Y. M. : They don't say what it is.
SECOND V. Y. M. : The intention is to thrill.
FIRST V. Y. M. (*reflectively*) : I've often wondered why so many amusements are controlled exclusively by housemaids.
SECOND V. Y. M. : Be fair. Housemaids don't write film sub-titles. These are done by retired charwomen.
FIRST V. Y. M. (*gloomily*) : Oh, well.

[*They relapse into silence. The lights in the big crystal chandeliers, on a hidden signal, fade gradually out, leaving the floor in darkness except for a dazzling pool of light at the platform end. The BAND is playing softly.*]

175

A FINANCIER: This is the vilest brandy in
Europe. I suppose they think you don't notice
it if you wear one of their false noses.

A BEAUTIFUL WOMAN (*listlessly*): You wanted
a cheery Christmas Eve.

THE FINANCIER: I expect my money's worth.

THE B. W. (*suddenly loathing him*): It screams
for it loudly enough.

> [*They are silent. The buzz of desultory chatter
> is still going on. The hands of the Louis
> Quinze clock under the music gallery point to
> a minute to twelve.*]

A GIRL WITH A CIGARETTE: Do look at the
Turkish-coffee johnny. Just behind us, here.
What an expression!

A YOUNG MAN IN AN EYEGLASS: Seeing
things.

> [*The red-fezzed* COFFEE-WAITER *in his gaudy
> uniform is standing bolt upright, his ebony
> features rigid and strained, with a look of
> expectation, mixed with wonder.*]

A BALDISH MAN: Tell you what he reminds
me of—a picture in Cologne, isn't it? Is it in
the cathedral or the museum? The Three Kings,
you know. He looks exactly like the black one.
Melchior, isn't it?

A FLUSHED YOUNG MAN: Talking of Cologne,
did I ever tell you the funny one about . . .

> [*His voice fades abruptly into silence, for a
> voice is singing. It is infinitely crystalline,
> ethereal, and distant, as if singing from a
> high tower. At the sound of it an indefinable*]

176

*breath sweeps over the hot and scented ball-
room.*]

THE VOICE (*singing*) : *Lux fulgebit hodie super
nos, quia natus est nobis Dominus.*

[*The pool of light grows more dazzling, golden,
and tremulous, wavering like a flame to the
roof.*]

THE VOICE (*as if from infinite distance*) : *Quia
natus est nobis Dominus.*

[*It is answered by a burst of music and many*
VOICES *singing together in unison.*]

VOICES : *Quia hodie descendit lux magna super
terram, alleluia.*
A SINGLE VOICE : *Videntes autem stellam,
gavisi sunt gaudio magno valde.*
VOICES : *A Domino factum est istud, et est
mirabile in oculis nostris, alleluia, alleluia.*

[*The light leaps up.*]

THREE VOICES (*in unison*) : *Vidimus enim
stellam ejus in Oriente, et venimus adorare eum.*
VOICES : *Jubilate Deo, omnis terra ; notum
fecit Dominus salutare suum, ante conspectum
gentium revelavit justitiam suam, alleluia, alleluia.*

[*A long silence.*]

VOICES (*dying away*) : *Alleluia.*

[*Silence. The light gradually assumes its former
shape and colour. The* GUESTS *at the Plaza
wake from a kind of frozen dream and
stare at each other dumbly, with questioning
eyes.*]

A STOUT FINANCIER (*approvingly*) : Not bad.

12   177

ON STRAW

A Lady in Pearls : No. . . . Get a waiter, will you ?

[*They order another magnum.*]

A Levantine Gentleman (*musing*) : Queer idea. Not as good as some of Solly's other efforts.

Another Levantine Gentleman : Quite new to have it done in Russian, though.

Third Levantine Gentleman : Think I'll book it, on spec.

[*They order another bottle.*]

A Girl with a Cigarette (*yawning*) : Kind of Impressionist stuff, what ?

A Flushed Young Man : What ? Yes. I was going to tell you about a funny thing happened in Cologne. George and I . . .

[*He tells it.*]

An Important Gentleman : I didn't care for the lighting. Was it Schwabe-Hasait ? Rather amateurish, anyway. Now Basil Dean . . .

[*Goes on boring.*]

A Very Pink Gentleman : What happens now ? Something really cheery, I hope.

[*A crash from the Band. The Chorus dancing in. They are dressed in white, as for toboganning. The divertissement (as advertised) is beginning at last, to the relief of a frenzied director.*]

The Very Pink Gentleman (*pensively*) : What I *do* say about this place is they give you decent food and don't tax your intelligence after it.

178

DIVERTISSEMENT

THE CHORUS (*dancing*) :

> *We are—wah—wah—wah—wah !*
> *So wah—wah—wah—wah—wah !*
> *We wah—wah—wah !*
> *And wah—wah—wah !*
> *Each wah—wah—wah—wah—wah !*

The cabaret continues.

EXPLICIT

PRINTED BY
JARROLD AND SONS LTD.
NORWICH

CPSIA information can be obtained
at www.ICGtesting.com
Printed in the USA
LVHW080848210323
742068LV00034B/1166